Praise for *Death, Immortality, and Resurrection*

With the measured tone of an experienced guide, Professor Vick introduces readers to the various landmarks surrounding the topics of death and immortality. He explores the major concepts of the future life, reviews both Greek and Biblical perspectives, and identifies a deeply personal relationship with God as the feature that gives the prospect of life after death its ultimate attraction.

Richard Rice, PhD
Professor of Religion
Loma Linda University

Edward Vick grapples with a subject that everyone wonders about at one time or another in his or her life: "Will I live after death, and will I be the same 'person' or know others?" To explore the question of immortality or resurrection after death, Vick examines the New Testament evidence, the views of philosophers like Plato, Aristotle, Descartes, John Hick, and Raymond Moody's book, Life After Life. He affirms that 'immortality' is God's gift to humanity. The real possibility of life after death involves, he believes, a belief in a certain kind of God that will initiate resurrection of the dead at the last day. Vick's book offers a challenging and rewarding read into a question on the minds of every person.

William Powell Tuck, ThD
Retired pastor and professor
Author of *The Journey to the Undiscovered Country*

Edward W. H. Vick's newest theological work enhances his reputation as a careful, analytical theologian who addresses the troubling questions believers and non-believers ponder. In this volume he explores the thorny issues of "death,""soul," "person," "death," consciousness after death, and the continuity of identity between our current existence and the next one. What is a "resurrection" or "spiritual" body? How is it like and how does it differ from the one we now possess? Can it be made intelligible to our modern ears steeped in physicality and materiality? Serious students of Scripture will be greatly helped in their quest for a profound understanding of these issues.

James J. Londis, PhD
Retired pastor and professor

In a time in which theologians and preachers claim either too much or too little about survival after death, Edward Vick presents an insightful vision of immortality as the gracious gift of a loving God. Vick surveys a variety of images of life after death in a clear and helpful manner and then presents a solidly biblical vision of resurrection. Vick blends solid academic research with accessibility for the lay reader. Regardless of your theological perspective, you will find this book to be an invaluable resource for imaging the afterlife. I highly recommend this text for individual or group study.

Bruce Epperly, PhD
Author of *From Here to Eternity: Preparing for the Next Adventure* and *Finding God in Suffering: A Journey with Job*

DEATH, IMMORTALITY, AND RESURRECTION

Edward W. H. Vick

Energion Publications
Gonzalez, Florida
2017

Copyright © 2017, Edward W. H. Vick

Unless otherwise noted, scripture quotations are from the Revised Standard Version of the Bible, copyright © 1946, 1952, and 1971 the Division of Christian Education of the National Council of the Churches of Christ in the United States of America. Used by permission. All rights reserved.

Scripture quotations marked NEB are taken from the New English Bible, copyright © Cambridge University Press and Oxford University Press 1961, 1970. All rights reserved.

Some translations are by the author.

ISBN10: 1-63199-267-8
ISBN13: 978-1-63199-267-4
Library of Congress Control Number: 2017933781

Energion Publications
P. O. Box 841
Gonzalez, FL 32560

energion.com
pubs@energion.com

Since I am coming to that holy room,
        Where, with thy choir of saints for evermore,
I shall be made thy music; as I come
        I tune the instrument here at the door,
        And what I must do then, think here before.

Whilst my physicians by their love are grown
        Cosmographers, and I their map, who lie
Flat on this bed, that by them may be shown
        That this is my south-west discovery
        Per fretum febris, by these straits to die,

I joy, that in these straits, I see my west;
        For, though their currents yield return to none,
What shall my west hurt me? As west and east
        In all flat maps (and I am one) are one,
        So death doth touch the resurrection.

Is the Pacific Sea my home? Or are
        The eastern riches? Is Jerusalem?
Anyan, and Magellan, and Gibraltar,
        All straits, and none but straits, are ways to them,
        Whether where Japhet dwelt, or Cham, or Shem.

We think that Paradise and Calvary,
        Christ's Cross, and Adam's tree, stood in one place;
Look Lord, and find both Adams met in me;
        As the first Adam's sweat surrounds my face,
        May the last Adam's blood my soul embrace.

So, in his purple wrapped receive me Lord,
        By these his thorns give me his other crown;
And as to others' souls I preached thy word,
        Be this my text, my sermon to mine own,
        Therefore that he may raise the Lord throws down.

                              John Donne
              Hymn to God my God, in my Sickness.

Table of Contents

Foreword..ix

PART I 1

I What Sort of Reality Is Death? 3
   1 We must all die..3
   2 Refusal...4
   3 Personal and universal...5
   4 The question..7
   5 The alternatives 12
   6 Our assumptions..13
   7 Speculation and revelation 14
   8 Soul and body 15
   9 The human person — a unity 17
   10 Resurrection...19

II The Teaching of the New Testament 23
   1 Pharisees and Sadducees 23
   2 Paul 24
   3 Bodily resurrection..25
   4 The death of Jesus and the death of the believer 30
   5 Jesus' resurrection and believers' resurrection 33
   6 The metaphor of sleep...37
   7 The interim state 41
   8 Concrete social relationships 44
   9 Person — the unity of a living being.........................46
   10 The proper subject of immortality?..........................49
   11 Eternal life 49

III Immortality and Other Words 51
   1 We value human life..51
   2 God bestows immortal life 52

   3 The finality of death...57
   4 Immortal life 58
   5 Various alternatives 61
   6 Meaning of *soul*..**64**
   7 God raises the dead 68
   8 God is immortal...69
   9 Four alternatives 72
   10 Four guiding considerations 75

IV Resurrection and Immortality..79
   1 Are they compatible?...79
   2 God takes the initiative 80
   3 Two kinds of language 81
   4 A qualitative difference 83
   5 Eternal life?..84

PART II 87
  Introduction 89
  V Plato...93
   1 Dualism..93
   2 The soul's knowledge and pre-existence..................94
   3 Ambiguity of the 'soul' 96
   4 Arguments for immortality..96
   5 *Meno:* Knowledge is remembering.......................**99**

  VI Aristotle's Functionalism...101
   1 Aristotle's question. 101
   2 Different kinds of activity 101
   3 Two Defining Statements..102
   4 Analogy of the eye 103
   5 Soul is not separable from body 104
   6 Aristotle's materialism..105
   7 Functions common and unique. 106

  VII Cartesian Dualism...107
   1 Man more than body...107

    2 The method of doubt 108
    3 Soul — the thinking thing 109
    4 Mind separate from body? 110
    5 Category mistake 111

VIII Replicas and Resurrection 115
    1 Imagining, reflecting, understanding 115
    2 Identity: Two meanings 116
    3 Replication 117
    4 Three pictures 120
    5 Qualitative identity 121

Additional Note 123

Index 129

Foreword

The subject of this book is immortality as the gift of God's grace, given as he wills. If immortality is God's gift, does everyone receive it? If not immediately, eventually? If God does not give it to everyone, what is the basis for granting it to some and not to others? Some? Are these the 'same' persons as have lived an earthly, mortal life? But what does 'same person' mean when used of the afterlife?

With widespread doubt and indifference about survival and the afterlife; with deliberate attempts in our society to isolate dying and death from life and consciousness, from the living and the conscious, it is essential that the Christian theologian bring home the importance, the opportunity and the tragedy of death. Before one can present the Christian hope, often in face of attractive alternative possibilities, the Christian must present the 'problem' of the reality of death.

The phrase 'conditional immortality' is an ambiguous one and not altogether happy. It needs clarification. We shall in fact use it hardly at all. In the course of our exposition we shall expound the following propositions:

1. God created man mortal.
2. Immortality is the gift of God's grace.
3. The soul is the person, not an element of the person, or the 'real person,' so the words 'soul' and 'person' are synonyms.
4. At death the person ceases to exist.
5. Unless the individual person who is restored to life is the same as the individual person who lived and died, the question of the immortality of the soul has no religious significance.
6. The restoration of life after death will be God's gracious gift, a new creative act.

7   God raises the dead and grants the person so raised immortality.

It is not always a good idea to read a book through just as it is written, although some readers may feel that they have to do that on principle. It is sometimes a good rule to start where you are most interested provided that you make certain allowances if you do so. Some people who will read this book will want to begin with the chapter on the teaching of the New Testament. Others may well want to start with Part Two, with the philosophical discussion. You should not feel that you *have* to start at the beginning, although that it not a bad place to start.

The author has written the book according to a specific plan and scheme of development, however. He hopes that as you read it, in your own way, the lines will converge and the unity of the treatment become clear. He hopes that the reader will have the satisfaction of renewed understanding and share some of the joy the author discovered (at times unexpectedly) for himself in thinking and writing about this age-old subject.

From time to time in the text we make reference to various quite fundamental philosophical teachings about the soul and immortality. But to ensure the flow of the argument, we do not explain such positions further or examine them in depth. In Part Two we engage in such philosophical discussions of soul, body, person, identity, survival.

There, we assess arguments for and against the dualism that separates body and soul, the dissoluble and the indissoluble, and arguments for the unity of the person. This supplements the specifically theological treatment of the first part of the book.

PART I

I What Sort of Reality Is Death?

1 We must all die

We only know life as we live it now. The life we now live is linked to a physical organism, the body. This body comes into being, grows and changes, comes to maturity, reaches the height of its powers. Then, it begins to deteriorate and finally it perishes. It is a relatively slow process, so that most people in reasonable health can adjust to it and prepare for the end that is inevitable. When we are young, we rejoice in the energies of the body, and when they gradually lessen we are reminded that one day there will be an end. Whatever developments in knowledge or growth in personality we achieve are accompanied by bodily experiences, bodily development. It's the body that finally succumbs, and the end of physical functions is the end of human life, as an active, developing, conscious, thinking thing. It may seem strange, perhaps unfortunate, that when a person has arrived at the stage of such mature experience, understanding and wisdom, and might continue to benefit themselves and others, his body lets him down and he must die. In fact, the situation has appeared so anomalous to some people that they have just not been able to reconcile themselves to it. They conclude that this life just cannot be the only life there is.

This does not necessarily mean that they are unhappy and discontented with this life. It is precisely because this life is so often satisfying that we feel that we cannot easily reconcile ourselves to the fact that we must abandon it. It is not only the weary and the oppressed, the unfortunate and the hopeless, who have longed for heaven and life beyond. When life smiles upon us and we bask in its sunshine and success, we feel we cannot let it go — not only for ourselves, but for other people, those whom we love in particular. If life is good, we would like to have it go on. If life is bad, we may feel it ought to be renewed and somehow be made good, if not now, then at some future time after death. Either way, we find it hard, passing strange, that life must end, that the bodily system, worn with the years of development and strain, should cease to function, that the end comes.

All of us must face the reality of death.

2 Refusal

But what sort of reality is it? What is the nature of the problem which we are going it discuss? We speak of *human* death. Since it is *man's* death and *man's* hope for what is beyond death that is the reality we are about to consider we must remind ourselves that it is not only human beings who die. We are not alone in our mortality. We are one with the animals and other living beings in this. We die. They die. But man is different. We can anticipate and prepare for death. We can shape our consciousness in acknowledgment and recognition of the fact that all our loves and hates will end with the dissolution of the body and the cessation of its function. It is not simply that we can make a will. It is also that our outlook, the consistency of our life, may be shaped and sobered by the fact that it all, one day, is to come to an end.

We may, of course, refuse to face this reality — that we will die. But it will not be because we do not know that death awaits all of us, ourselves included. It is because the thought of death is a kind of insolence, an unwelcome impertinence, an uncouthness in the midst of life. So it must be repressed. The fact of death must be made as little obvious as possible. The reality of death must be camouflaged and tinted. Death is not welcome. It is an intruder. It is not a friend but an enemy. So, in our modern society, we shut it from us. We hide the dying from view. We speak in euphemisms. Death is a passing away, a sleep. We save our most expensive and strangely beautiful gifts of flowers to soften for us the impact of the ugliness of death. The fact that fewer people die early in life than used to be the case, and that we are not likely to be involved in the deaths of so many, if any, young persons and children today, as compared to say a hundred years ago, means that we do not have brought home to us the stark inevitability of death. But even when we know, we try to fool ourselves. Even worse, we try to fool the dying. 'We act and we lie, as if by so doing we could change the reality of death into something temporary, something even pleasant; as if by playing the act, we could change the human relationship and make good the years of wasted opportunities. We rearrange the surface and fool ourselves that we have stirred the depths. Such is the inauthenticity with which we greet the prospect of death when we see that we can by no means avoid it. Nothing may have changed in our relations to the dying, but we can pretend they have. We can then perhaps salve our own conscience for lost opportunities in the past, and hope to deceive the dying. But are we really fooled? The tragedy is that we may be and that death becomes trivialised and banal. So Tolstoy could write of Ivan Ilych, and in doing so wrote of himself. 'The awful, terrible act of his dying was, he could see, reduced by those about him to the level of a casual, unpleasant and almost indecorous incident ... and this was done by that very decorum which he had served all his life long ... This falsity around him and within him did more than anything else to poison his last days.'[1]

The twofold answer to our question, 'What sort of reality is death?' then, is that death is a personal reality: I will die. It is also a universal reality. All human beings die.

3 Personal and universal

Death is a personal reality. I am the one who will die. I am the one who is involved because of the dying and death of someone I love.

Death is a personal reality. There is all the difference between holding that the proposition 'All men must die' is true, and com-

---

1 Leo Tolstoy, *The Death of Ivan Ilych and Other Stories*. London: Oxford University Press, 1971, pp. 51,52.

ing to recognise that this life which I love and enjoy, with its light and colour and shade, must and will come to an end. Since this is so, we shall (if we live honestly and with frankness) live the life we now have in view of the fact that it will one day end. That makes a difference. I come to terms with myself when I can reckon with my life *in view of its end*. If I only have so much, how shall I not reckon with what I have? It is wisdom, honesty and authenticity that I do. Life takes on a depth it would otherwise lack if I reckon *realistically* with the fact of death. Obsession is a fanaticism and the opposite kind of inauthenticity. Death must be reckoned with in the midst of life. It is then that the living takes on a meaning it would otherwise lack. The realisation of the brevity of life lends an intensity to life it would without such realisation not have. I well remember an interview with an aging writer. 'I treasure,' she said, 'this springtime, and I value the sight of the new violets.' 'I think,' she went on, 'that these might be the last spring violets that I shall see. So I love them more than ever.'

There is a certain conscious intensity to life when one values it, brief as it is. This is no illusion, no sentimentality, for one is facing, rather than retreating from, life.

The fact is that a Christian believer can look without illusions to the fact of his death and his dying. He looks to God who is revealed in a dying and a death — the death of Jesus. It is in the light of this important fact, the fact that God is revealed in the death of Jesus, that we may find resources to approach the task of living in view of life's end, the task of dying. The Christian will consider what sort of reality death is in view of the dying of Jesus.

For it is to a cross that the Christian looks when he thinks of God, and it is to a resurrection that his attention is directed when he knows the reality of death. It has been from the very beginning. The earliest of the formal creeds connected together the important beliefs of Christian faith in one short statement: 'I believe in God ... and in Jesus Christ ... who ... was crucified, dead and buried. He descended into hell. The third day he rose again from the dead. I believe in the resurrection of the body and

Death, Immortality, and Resurrection

the life everlasting.' Death is reckoned with as a central article in the Christian's creed. To be a Christian means to reckon seriously with the fact of death. While doing so, the Christian is a theist. He believes in God, that is to say. So he can connect God with the fact of death. He can construct a theology of death. If Christian faith is to be meaningful, it will support the realities with which life is lived, when a human being has become aware of the fact that he will, must, die. It will not provide a flight from reality, a pie-in-the-sky-when-you-die kind of pseudo-comfort. Living is too serious and too good a business to be diverted permanently by frivolities. It is one of the tests of genuine Christian faith that it supports real life and realistic living.

4 THE QUESTION

Since death is both a personal and a universal reality, we can put the problem in two ways. It was expressed by Job in the conditional sentence, 'If a man die, shall he live again?' (*Job* 14:14). There are different ways of expressing the meaning of this conditional.

If all human beings were to die, if the human race ceased to exist, would that be the end of human life? If the curtain comes down on us all, would human existence cease for ever? As long as human beings can propagate human beings, there is hope for the continuance of human life. But does it make any sense to talk about *human* life when all human beings have died? Is it rational to entertain such a hope? Does theistic faith, belief in God as Creator, as Ultimate and as Love, give us ground for hope?

The second way of putting the question is the personal one. If I die, is that the end of my human life? Is it possible that there will be a taking up of the threads again after my death? If so, will the renewal be in any sense *human*? Can I, an individual, hope for the continuance of what I here and now value so much? Does the Christian faith provide us with special resources to answer this question?

It is, of course, possible that all human beings will not die. It is possible that I shall not die. But we would then have to ask whether the conditions now prevailing would in due time be changed. So the problem of continuity would remain.

We could put the meaning of Job's question, 'If a man die, shall he live again?' in another way. We learn most of our meanings through experience. We know what 'being a father' means by being fathers. We know what being in pain, winning a game, following a trail, finding a treasure, solving a problem etc. mean by going through the appropriate experience. How can we know what sort of reality death is unless we live on beyond it, so that we can assess the significance of the death which we have died? For we can only understand the meaning of what happens to us, it seems, when we have a point from which we can see it in the setting of our whole existence. We understand the meaning of something in our experience, say an illness, a birth, a failure, as we look back on it and assess it in the light of other personal events. As life goes on we may well assess different events differently as our perspectives change with what we like to call maturity. Our autobiography will be written differently at one time than another. But, in any event, we must be able to look back and to integrate one experience with the rest of our experience. 'I can tell you how listening to that talk made a decisive difference to my whole life,' you may say as you look back on the whole of your life so far, within which that experience is integrated. But you cannot say, 'My death made a real difference to my whole life.'

I received a very interesting letter this week. The opening sentence was particularly striking. It is obvious that someone had made a mistake somewhere. 'I was sorry to learn of the death of your mother, but am pleased to hear that she will be able to come and live near you.' As you can imagine, I had to read that sentence again before I realised what my good friend had intended to say. He was not making an exception in this case, nor had he got his or the human experience about death wrong — or at least, I am assuming with some certainty that he had not. Just that between the

Death, Immortality, and Resurrection

dictation and the typing a human error had constructed a perfectly grammatical sentence. We can, of course, integrate the experience of someone else's death into our own experience. But we cannot integrate our own. So if to be able to understand death we must be able to look back on it, it seems that we cannot answer our question in that way.

An interesting book,[2] which raised a great deal of interest, discussed the possibility of looking back after death, or at least after what comes very near to being dead. One cannot interview the dead, since death is not a part of human experience. But some people have had unusual experiences when, at the point of death and in circumstances when they could have been expected to die, they felt themselves to be out-of-the-body. They returned to ordinary life after the crisis and told of their experience. Is what happened to them and their description of it relevant to our question, 'If a man die, shall he live again?' I do not believe that it assists to answer this question, as our comments in Part Two of this book will make clear.

There is simply no looking back after death.

Significant events and movements in history are understood in retrospect. Some lives, some events, some deaths are seen to be specially important as they are related to other events in a series. We can co-ordinate other peoples' deaths with ongoing events in history, because we are the survivors. So it is that history is written.

But there is no retrospect with reference to my death, nor with reference to the death of 'all men.' There is no retrospect for me if it is the end of my human life, nor if it is the end of all human life. So how can I know whether my life or my death *is* significant, and if it is significant, what that significance is, if I do not survive it? Since death is the cessation of life, it would plainly seem that there is no *survival*. If one survives an accident, then one lives to tell the tale. If he does not survive then it must be told by someone else. One recalls the last words of Hamlet. After life has been lived, 'the rest is silence.' Death is non-survival. Death is, by definition, the end. But we find it very hard to leave it at that. Death, we accept

---

2 Raymond A, Moody, *Life After Life*. New York: Bantam Books, 1976.

is the end. But is it the end of *everything*? Death is cessation. But is there no continuity of anything? Nothing at all?

It is an obvious enough fact that when we die, the bodily functions cease, that at death this body decays and goes to dust, that its particles are assimilated into other realities. There is no question of the reality of physical dissolution. That is real and inescapable enough. On that level the question about death is answered. It is the end. The brain, the respiration and the heart cease to function. Death means the irreparable ceasing of all bodily functions.

But the question that has puzzled people is not about the physical functions. It is not a matter of asking whether, once the physical functions have stopped they can be made to start again. We know the answer to that question. With death physical dissolution is non-reversible. That is the point at which we *begin* to ask the question that bothers us. *Given* this physical dissolution, what of the reality of death? It is when we have given our definition of death as the ceasing of bodily functions that we begin to ask about its reality. When we know, as we do, that physically there is no return, it is then we ask the question, 'What is death?' Is there more to human life and death than an end in bodily dissolution?

We have already, in one sense, answered the question. Death is the end of physical life, the cessation of bodily functions. What are we doing then, if having already given this answer, we go on pressing the question? Is it unwarranted to define death as the end, and then to suggest that the definition is inadequate? To pursue the question when we have already given this answer does not mean that we are not taking the answer seriously. We are reflecting on how seriously we are going to take that answer — namely, that death is the end. Is there any way of maintaining that even though it is the end, death is not the end. 'To be or not to be?' that *is* the question. Shall we be, after we are not?

We are not simply playing with words, but are raising an important issue. We can put it in terms of a paradox, as the last question suggested. But the point is that we are often not satisfied that death as physical dissolution is the end of the human story. When the medical man has pronounced his verdict, is there something important for the believer and the theologian to say? If science speaks about death on one level, is there another level of *significant* talk about it?

We may wish at this point simply to plead ignorance and close the discussion. We know what death is, in the sense that we have experienced the dying and the death of our fellows, someone whom we have loved and cherished, perhaps. We know the difference it has made. So we know what death means, and we assume that it will have some such meaning for those who know and love us when it will be our death. But beyond that we do not press and we do not desire to press. We have gone as far as our experience allows us and we go no further. So we are ready to let the matter rest.

But nevertheless we may find that at times we have our doubts about such an attitude. We may be content to let it rest when it is a question of our own survival. But are we quite ready to do so when it is someone whom we have loved, and who has loved us. 'Loved long since,' we say, and then somewhat wistfully perhaps, 'and lost *awhile*?' We may not get beyond this wistfulness. We have a vague hope that there might be something pleasant, an inarticulate fear that all may not be well, or an uncertain hunch that death marks the final end. We do not know. We cannot be certain. So we try to live above our vague hope, our inarticulate fear or our scepticism. We immerse ourselves in the business of life.

We may, if we take this attitude, find that the important problem is that of dying well. The reality of death is to reckon with the fact that I must die, to come to terms with it. Dying is the last bit of living I do, carrying on the business of living well right to the end. As we live, so we die. I see to it that, in view of my death, in view of my having to die, *now* I shall live well. I see to it that in view of my having lived well, I shall die well. The important thing is living well — right to the end. That's the most important thing, rather than being concerned about what comes after, if anything does.

We live in a time and culture in which it is not considered proper to speak frankly and openly about dying and about death.

We may speak professionally about it. Or we may laugh about it because we cannot take it seriously. We shield ourselves from the reality of death and we isolate the dying ones from us. So it is even a sign of robustness and of health that we can be speaking about living in view of our dying. It is a symptom of authenticity that we speak seriously about death.

But this is not enough to express the belief and the hope of the Christian believer in God. The Christian believer lives his life and thinks his thoughts in relation to God's revelation of himself in Jesus Christ. His Christian faith shows itself to be adequate by illuminating all aspects of his experience. Christians seek to bring two facts together, the fact of faith and the fact of death. Given the reality of death and given the reality of Christian faith in God, what may we say of death? What may we say of death in face of the central reality and symbol of Christian faith, the dying and the death of Jesus on a cross? That cross is the symbol, whose meaning we must explore in view of our own prospects. In view of the death we shall die, what shall we say of the death Jesus died? In view of the fact that Jesus died, what shall we say of the death we shall die?

5 THE ALTERNATIVES

So we can now return to our question. In view of the acknowledged dissolution of the physical organism, the body, what alternatives present themselves as logical possibilities? A logical possibility is one we can think of without contradiction. So we can consider it reasonably. Whether it is an actual possibility will depend upon other than logical considerations. Several logical possibilities are worth considering. We shall simply state them here and in due course explore whether Christian faith can be readily and consistently expressed through them.

First, a non-physical entity with which the real self is identified persists, either disembodied or re-incarnated in another body. Second, there is an impersonal survival, in the memory of other persons, in historical influence, or in God. What we have been and

Death, Immortality, and Resurrection

what we have done lives on. Third, there is no further consciousness. Death is the end of the body and of all consciousness. Fourth, there is conscious, personal survival, but in a form which is quite different from this life. Fifth, the body is recreated, or a body is newly created so that there is identity between the person who died and the person who will live again.

Here a crucial and fundamental problem arises. On what basis may we make judgments about such alternative possibilities? The difficulty is that of how we may possibly decide either to accept one of these alternatives, or to reject them all, convinced that we cannot know the answer and that all talk about such a state after death is idle.

6 OUR ASSUMPTIONS

It is time to state assumptions. First, the matter is worth pursuing. This is not merely an academic exercise, in which one can hold aloof from the subject matter, as if the subject of the discussion were remote from the personal interest. The answers given to the question matter to us as persons. Second: the Christian takes his bearings from the revelation of God in Jesus Christ, his death and his resurrection. For our present undertaking, this means that we shall try to connect faith in the resurrection of Jesus Christ with both the fact of death, the one certain, supremely tragic, universal, inescapable fact; and with our questions about what lies beyond death. Third: what we then say must be reasonable. That means that it must be intelligible. We must attempt to give a reasoned, consistent and coherent account of our Christian convictions. Otherwise we shall be endorsing and proposing we know not what. So we shall have to keep asking ourselves the question, 'What do we mean by what we say we believe?' That is a difficult thing to do. But if we persist, we shall come to a clarity which will be a credit to our faith. So — to repeat the question — how shall we decide?

It is of course, not only the Christian who has asked the question about death. It is a *human* question, since death is universal.

So people everywhere have left traces of their concern about death, and have tried to come to terms with it. This means that some of what is said will be of philosophical interest. Not everything that has been said about death will be of *religious* interest. We shall, later, ask what makes the difference.

7 Speculation and revelation

There are, for the concerned inquirer, two possible ways of coming to the question, of engaging the reason, of providing guidance, in the discussion. One way is the way of *speculation*, the way of philosophy. So the efforts of the philosophers to understand the problem of death have produced concepts and arguments well worth careful consideration. Without clear concepts one cannot adequately state and come to grips with a problem. Without meaningful propositions and sound arguments one cannot come to reasoned and reasonable conclusions. The concepts which make this discussion possible, meaningful, and interesting were forged on philosophical anvils. These are such concepts as soul, immortality, body, dualism, eternity, everlasting, person, unity, continuity, identity, spirit, mind, reality, idea, form, existence, reincarnation. Since such ideas have been adopted by Christian writers, these and other concepts which appear in these pages have had both a secular philosophical history, as well as a Christian one. One way of proceeding would be to look at the background of these ideas and the propositions and arguments which present them.

The other way, we may call the way of *revelation*. Here the claim is made that there is a place in the long course of human history where God has made himself known. For the Christian, God has revealed himself in Jesus Christ. In view of that revelation, what may we say about the problem of death?

We do not, on principle, have to set these two ways in opposition to each other. After all you cannot get very far in stating the issues without making use of the concepts listed above. Why may it not be the case, since reason is a God-given gift, that we

Death, Immortality, and Resurrection

may sometimes discover that thinkers have used it to come to right conclusions, even if they have not been directly illuminated by the light which has issued from the revelation of God in Jesus Christ?

The theologian's task is to reason well in the interests of Christian faith, to engage in a process of questioning and constructing, which involves examining and assessing past constructions. It is by such a process of thoughtful interpretation that one arrives at a considered and reasonable conclusion. For the Christian, the constant reference point will be the revelation of God in Jesus Christ, attested in the New Testament. What happens when considering the question of death and immortality, as in other areas of theology, is that the Christian, trying to understand what he believes, receives help in his quest for understanding from other people who have devoted themselves to the pursuit of truth before him. He will sometimes learn from their errors. He will often learn from their truths. In the process he will come to have discernment for himself. So we shall try to learn what lessons we can from those who have gone before us and have left us their concepts, propositions, reasoning and conclusions. People of all ages thought about the fact of death and have wondered and questioned, 'What is man?' So the question of the relation of soul to body arose.

We have on this page now made reference to two important concepts, both of which have a long history, namely, *immortality* and *soul*. Is the body a kind of prison in which the soul is housed for a while, but which at length dissolves, and in so doing liberates the soul for its free, untrammelled existence?

8 Soul and body

To speak of soul as something quite different from body, and to set the two against each other as opposites is known as *dualism*, the word for the opposition, the dichotomy, of two contrasting realities. Dualism of soul and body provides one answer to the question, 'What is man?' Dualism states that man is soul, but has a body. The body is the inhibiting factor for the soul's expression.

The soul inhabits the body. The body inhibits the soul. The body is the prison of the soul.

It was in pursuit of such questions that some Greeks came to the conclusion that the soul is immortal, and Plato, in particular, provided several interacting arguments from which he drew his conclusion. But he had not been the first to speak of a non-physical reality which lived on after the death of the body. Indian religious teachers and sages had taught that the soul not only lives on after the body but also lived before it. The doctrine of re-incarnation has for its foundation the belief that the soul is immortal.

If the soul is immortal and the body dies, the soul will outlive the body. If it is necessary that there be a body through which the soul expresses itself, then the soul must be 'reborn' into a new body at the death of the old one. The process could be interminable, and one not to be anticipated. For if no progress is made after interminable deaths and rebirths, how could one but be pessimistic or despairing at the prospect?

The Platonic idea of the soul's separateness and otherness from the body[3] persisted. In the early Christian centuries, Christians attempted to come to terms with such teachings about the soul. The fact is that the doctrine that the soul is immortal became widely accepted among Christians and was held as orthodox Christian teaching for centuries. But, widespread acceptance and persistence of an idea are no guarantee of its truth. Consensus provides psychological support for accepting teachings. When people are happily inclined to endorse an opinion anyway, such consensus makes it compelling. Human beings are quite happy to accept the proposal that death is not the end. The teaching of the immortality of the soul became accepted as official Christian teaching. Such teaching assumed that the soul was a reality distinct from the body.

The Christian teaching of the soul's immortality said more than simply that the soul survived the body and lived on endlessly. There may be little comfort in that. In fact, it could be repellent and frightening. The immortality of the soul was related to Christian

---

3   See chapter VI below.

Death, Immortality, and Resurrection 17

teaching about God, and about ethics. The kind of life after death, while it will be a gift of God, depends upon the sort of life one had lived in this mortal existence.

The doctrine of the immortality of the soul, accepted by Christian teachers, was supported by the venerable philosophical arguments of Plato. It thus became well secured for centuries of Christian belief, both on the authority of the church and of the reasoning of the philosophers.

Is it supported by science? Does science help us in considering the fact of death, of the soul, of survival? Social and psychological science can provide us with statistical assessments, and judgments concerning death as a social and individual phenomenon. Its comparative studies enable us to make predictions about life expectancy, for example. Such sorts of study have little to contribute to an answer to the kind of question we are asking, 'What sort of reality is death?'

Is there scientifically acceptable evidence to establish the fact of life after death? Can one appeal, for example, to well-attested accounts of out-of-the-body experiences as evidence for the existence of the soul and for the persistence after death of a non-physical reality? Can the so-called psychic phenomena be plausibly interpreted as conclusively indicating life after death? In reference to such phenomena there is room for scientific appraisal, even if it turns out that the scientist is puzzled and prefers to reserve his judgment. But there need be no undue fear or expectation in relation to such findings on the part of the Christian believer.

9 THE HUMAN PERSON — A UNITY

One certain result of the modern understanding is that the traditional dualism which separated soul and body and defined man in terms of that dichotomy is not acceptable. We do not find a spiritual essence housed in a body, a 'ghost in the machine.' Human consciousness is not known apart from the body. A human being is a psycho-somatic unity. We must assume such unity in all our discussion about death, established as it is by our modern understanding. Man is a unity and his spiritual and personal life is indissolubly tied to its physical base. What shall we conclude from this fact? Does it bear upon our consideration of the problem of survival? Can we, if we deny the existence of soul as a spiritual entity within us, then decide whether or not there is further life when the body comes to its end? Does the fact that our psycho-somatic unity is dissolved by death mean that the death of the body is the end of us? Here opinions differ. One contemporary writer has observed. 'To many moderns, the Old Testament dictum, "dust thou art, and unto dust shalt thou return" (*Genesis* 3:19 K.J.V.), seems more likely true than the Greek hopes of immortality that informed many centuries of Christian belief.'[4] That is a quite unexceptionable statement. The question is: What follows from this? Does it follow that because man is a psycho-physical unity, that the end of the body, therefore, is the end of the man, except to the degree that our ideas, attitudes and actions continue to affect the communities and cultures within which he lived and worked? Is it the case that our life, our consciousness, ceases totally and so eternally at death, that death marks the ultimate end of the person, except as one's influence continues?

Let us suggest another solution. Death is the end of man, except that God in some creative activity of his grace shall act to make renewed life possible. This alternative possibility suggests that the dissolution of the unity which is the human which takes place at death marks an end, a decisive end. While decisive, however, it is not an ultimate end. If we can give good grounds for believing that there is a possibility of life after death, after the dissolution of the psycho-somatic unity which now constitutes the human, we shall have provided a reasonable alternative to the idea that death marks man's ultimate dissolution.

---

4 Gordon P. Kaufman, *Systematic Theology. A Historicist Perspective*. New York: Charles Scribners Sons, 1968. p. 464.

If we define the human by our present experience we would have to say that in the absence of the body the human person cannot exist. At death the human person ceases to be. He returns to the dust. No soul takes its flight to other fields than these earthly ones. There is no such soul to take such flight. The psycho-somatic unity which is the human person no longer exists at death. The human person ceases to be, passing from being to non-being. What we have been, we now no longer are. The unity which constitutes our human life ceases at death. We are thus faced with two alternatives: that this cessation is the end of the human, or that it is not. Is it possible that while our consciousness ceases at death, that is not the end of all human consciousness?

To agree that the dissolution of the personality and the cessation of the consciousness occur at death does not prohibit us from holding, in opposition to a teaching of *total* extinction at death, the possibility of restoration of life, of renewal of consciousness. It does not prohibit us from exploring the meaning of resurrection. That is a clear logical possibility. In fact, it clears the ground for us, so that we do not have to attempt the impossible task of reconciling the idea of resurrection with that of the innate immortality of the soul.

10 Resurrection

The question 'If a man die, shall he live again?' is still open, given the dissolution of the personality and cessation of human being at death. An alternative to the theory of extinction is that of resurrection. God raises the dead. What are the grounds for believing that God will provide for a continuance of life, in continuity with the life we have known here? It is certainly a valid logical possibility and it must therefore be given due consideration as an alternative to the extinction theory on the one hand and the theory of the immortality of the soul on the other hand.

Consider the two arguments:

(1) Death dissolves the unity which is the human person.

Therefore death is the end of man.

(2) The human person is a psycho-somatic unity.
Therefore, since death dissolves this unity, death is the end, unless God shall act to restore man to life.
God so acts
Therefore there is life after death.

If the conclusion of (2) is valid, we will have to reckon with an interim period or state between death and restoration in which there is no consciousness, no life.

There can be no question of proof. What Christians claim about the reality of and the possibility of life after death will be based upon God's revelation in Jesus Christ. Christian theology seeks to interpret this event as faithfully as possible.

The appeal to revelation in this case involves the following claims. (1) There is a place in human existence where death has not been final. (2) Such a place is not isolated, but is *typical*, or as we might say, *germinal*. It has consequences beyond the individual case. It represents and at the same time makes possible what it represents, namely that death is not final. From the fact that death was not final in the case of Jesus Christ has resulted the fact that death is not final for man. (3) This activity of God in Jesus Christ, known as the resurrection, is the ground for Christian hope of life after death and provides the decisive clue to the activity of God we can expect.

The Christian tradition has not always *realised* its resources. In the case of its teaching about death it attempted to express its hope in terms of the Platonic notion of the immortality of the soul. That led to inconsistencies, for example, if the soul is the essence of man and is released at death to enter into its real existence, which it enjoys immediately after death, what need, or 'room' is there for a resurrection of the body at the last day, a teaching which was also strongly affirmed in Christian doctrine.

But now, when for good reasons, we reject such a teaching of the existence of the soul, we can re-appraise traditional Christian thinking about death and about life after death. We may do so by setting aside the Platonic teaching of the immortality of the soul, but we shall not do so without examining the arguments for immortality (see Additional Note 2a). But where those arguments assume the entity called 'soul,' they are vulnerable to an empirical check. If there is no evidence for the existence of an entity different from the body and housed within it, we can and shall reject the idea of the soul *in that sense*.

This does not mean that we may not reasonably there speak of immortality. Nor does it mean that we may not use the term 'soul.' It may be that we can even talk of the 'immortality of the soul.' But if we do, it will not be in the dualistic sense, i.e. of a reality that can exist within the body and apart from the body. If we cannot speak of the soul *in this way*, then we cannot mean by the immortality of the soul the survival of an entity separable from body and something other than the person. What terms shall we use to express ourselves?

II The Teaching of the New Testament

1 Pharisees and Sadducees

Many different beliefs about death and what is beyond were current among the Jews of the first century. The Sadducees believed in extinction at death. There was 'no resurrection, nor angel, nor spirit.' The Essenes taught the immortality of the soul, as did the Greeks. The Qumran Covenants, it seemed, believed in resurrection, but not of the present body. The Pharisees believed in a bodily resurrection at the end or history. 'The Pharisees acknowledge them all 'that is angels, resurrection and spirit' (*Acts* 23:8).

Similarly, as Christians began to think about death and the afterlife, there was also to be found a considerable variety of opinion. It is an interesting fact that the teachings we find in first century Judaism are also, in due time, to be taught in the Christian church. What happened after death was often among the Jews a hotly disputed issue, as Sadducees and Pharisees came into conflict with one another. Jesus clearly took the position that the life to come would be a different form than this one. The level of consciousness, to use our earlier term, would be different from this one.

So, the Pharisees were wrong to see the resurrection life, as for all intents and purposes, a continuation of this one. The argument of the Sadducees showed the absurdity of thinking of resurrection life as being just like this one, with sex and family life. The Sadducees told the story of a woman who outlived seven husbands (*Mark* 12:18-22). They then asked about the state of her married life in the hereafter, when the lot of them would live again. The Sadducees, who did not believe in the resurrection of the dead, thought that the consideration of this case showed how absurd it was to think in Pharisaic terms, over-literally, about the next life.

When they told this story of the woman who married seven husbands in all to Jesus he rebuked them. God is the God of the living, not of the dead, and his power must be reckoned with. Jesus said to them, 'Is not this why you are wrong, that you know neither the Scripture nor the power of God. For when they rise from the dead, they neither marry nor are given in marriage, but are like angels in heaven' (*Mark* 12:24,25).

The Sadducees were wrong for failing to take account of the power of God, who would raise the dead. The Pharisees were wrong for thinking that the resurrection life would be like this one. But they were right to hold a belief in resurrection. Jesus shared this belief with them, but not in their crassly materialistic way.

2 Paul

Paul was a Pharisee. He believed in the resurrection. But he did not believe it so naively as to think that it was simply a continuation of life in the body as we know it in this existence. He is most reluctant to do any more than to *assert* that there will be a resurrection of the body. He considers the possibility that there are different kinds of body. There are bodies of fish, of birds and animals and they are not the same. Why should there not be a different sort of body than the physical body which human beings have? Why not speak of a 'spiritual body' in contrast to a 'physical body'? So he asserts that like the seed of corn is different from the cob or the plant it produces, the resurrection body is different from the body that is, so to speak, sown into the earth. Paul is not constructing an argument, but trying out an illustration. So he says, 'It is sown a physical body, it is raised a spiritual body. If there is a physical body, there is also a spiritual body' (*I Corinthians* 15:44.) What dies is the physical body. What is raised is the spiritual body. He than makes an explicit denial: 'I tell you this, brethren (words used to emphasise what he is about to say): flesh and blood cannot inherit the kingdom of God, nor does the perishable inherit the imperishable' (v. 50).

Death, Immortality, and Resurrection

A contrast is drawn sharply between this existence and the resurrection existence. This existence is 'flesh and blood.' It is perishable. But man will not remain as he now is. Paul here intends to indicate a fundamental difference between existence in this life and existence in the life to come. This is quite in harmony with what he says elsewhere: 'While we are *at home in* the body we are *away from* the Lord ... we would rather be *away from* the body and at home with the Lord' (*II Corinthians* 5:6-8.)

3 Bodily resurrection

We must make an important distinction here, since we can do justice to this teaching only as we do so. Paul speaks of bodily resurrection. He also distinguishes the resurrection body from the body of this existence. So we can, and must, carefully distinguish between resurrection of the flesh and resurrection of the body.

When earlier Christian teachers talked of the 'resurrection of the flesh' they meant that the very same matter which composed the flesh of the human individual would be reconstituted at the resurrection and the identical physical structure would be restored. The whole body would be reconstituted at the resurrection, no matter how its parts had been dispersed.

The doctrine of the resurrection of the flesh, as it was called, has a long ancestry in Christian belief. It may be said to represent a consensus for the greater part of Christian faith up to the present. The doctrine maintains that at the resurrection, the identical body which died will be restored to life again. It will be constituted by the identical particles which made up that body which once lived. They thought that only if the identical particles were restored to the individual pattern which prevailed in the physical body of the one who had lived could the identity of the individual be guaranteed. If he is to be the same person, he had to have the same body after death he had before death.

An early statement found in Augustine recognises the difficulties but holds that the power of the Creator will overcome them.[5] Even if bodies are eaten by wild beasts or by cannibals, or have disintegrated, God will 'revive them all and restore them to life.' In the case of the cannibal, he says that 'flesh will he restored to the man in whom it first began to be human flesh!' But he does have his reservations. The resurrected body may ot be identical with the body that died. The body of the resurrection will be the mature body, a beautiful and proportionate body. Augustine does not oppose the view that the person will rise 'with the precise stature he had when he departed this life,' but claims that all ugliness, weakness, sluggishness, corruption will disappear from it. Whatever has happened to the living body, even if 'it has ceased to be an entity in any particular place,' it is not beyond the 'power of the Almighty Creator' to reassemble the identical particles, so that not a hair of its head will perish, that is to say, so that the exact same body will be restored.' Even if that flesh had completely disappeared and none of its material remained in any cranny of the natural world, the Almighty would reproduce it from whatever source he chose. Even if it did not exist, God would make it exist. It is obviously very difficult to understand how it could then be called the same flesh. Was Augustine prepared to go to such lengths because he was convinced that to be the same person one had to have the identical body at different times?

But, is physical identity a necessary condition for identity of the person? If it is not, is a concept of resurrection appropriate? For example would replication be resurrection? Replication entails that God produce an identical person in a different body.

We feel that personal identity is a necessary condition when it is a question of apportioning praise, blame, reward, and punishment. If we wish to punish the wrong doer and reward the right doer, we must be quite sure that we bestow what is merited upon the same person who did the evil or the good.

---

5 *City of God*. XXII. 20.

In the New Testament the resurrection is directly related to the apportioning of rewards and punishments. There is a 'first resurrection' and a 'second death' (*Revelation* 20:6), 'the resurrection of life' and 'the resurrection of judgment,' the former for those who have done good, the latter for those who have done evil (*John* 5:18-19). There will be a reward for those who do good, 'on the day when good men rise from the dead' (*Luke* 14:14). The vision of the Apocalypse presents two resurrections, separated by a period of a thousand years. At the beginning there is the first resurrection, in which the blessed are renewed to life and begin to 'reign' with Christ. The 'rest of the dead' do not rise until the end of the millennium and then their rebellion is quelled by destructive fire which produces the 'second death' from which there is no return. (*Revelation* 20:4-10). Thus are the good and the bad rewarded: one by an eternal punishment (that is, a punishment whose effects are eternal), the other by eternal life. Something similar is taught in the parable of the sheep and the goats (*Matthew* 25:31-46). All receive their due in accordance with what they have done in this earthly life. Those who have done justly will be rewarded. Those who have done unjustly will be punished.

This assumes an identity between the person that was and the person who is raised from the dead. How shall this identity be preserved? One way in which we now ensure identity is by noting and recognizing physical characteristics which are unique and which sometimes cannot be changed. So if we have doubt about a person's identity we can examine the distinguishing features which they bear physically. We look at the fingerprints. We look at the eye scan. We look for the birthmarks and other unique bodily features. These remain and distinguish one from other persons. Such features do not change, and so they can serve to identify one as that particular person. On recognizing the features we usually have no doubt who he or she is, even if we have not seen that person for many years. But identity of physical features is not all that the Christian writers, to whom we have referred, meant when they spoke of the 'resurrection of the flesh.' They believed what is plainly impossible.

When we recognise a person as the same person we knew because we observe the same physical features we knew before, we are certainly not saying and do not believe that the particles which make up the body now are the same particles which made it up, say, six or seven years ago. Seven years on, not one particle in my body now will be in my body then. But I shall still insist that, other things being equal, I am the *same person*. I think that if you had known me years ago and I you, but we had not met for several years, we would have quite clear ways of establishing that you are the same person I knew and I am the same person you knew. But it would be quite unnecessary, as well as being impossible, to establish that every particle in my body was the same as it was then.

'God raises the dead' was taken by the Christian writers to whom we have referred to mean that the identical physical particles were, at the resurrection, brought together to reconstitute the same physical body as existed during the earthly life. We have seen that this is both impossible and also unnecessary to preserve the identity of the person. We must distinguish this from the belief that at the resurrection God raises the dead by creating an exact 'replica' of the person who died.[6] While there are difficulties with this view, it does not fall into the gross errors of the other.

In the end, if we are to be faithful to the Pauline position we will choose between two understandings: that the body of the resurrection will be either the earthly body transformed, or a new 'heavenly' body bestowed by God, and re-embodying the personality which once was. On the latter view the physical body, the person, perishes at death. But at the resurrection, God recreates the person, continuous (yet also discontinuous) with the person that was. For in creating a reproduction or 'replica,' God brings into being a new life. It is a new life in consideration of the life which once was, and it has the capacity to exist in a new environment. It has a life appropriate to a 'new heavens and a new earth,' which God also creates. There is thus both continuity with what was,

---

6 This view, expounded and defended by John Hick, is discussed in chapter XI below.

and there is what is new, that which enables the recreated person to live his renewed existence under the new conditions. What that existence or that body will be like, we cannot say. We remember that Paul was also unable to say. When we speak of God's creative act, we are brought to the limits of our understanding.

The only life we know is life in the body. So the term 'bodily life' is something of a repetition. The New Testament speaks of the resurrection of believers in bodily terms. When we try to expatiate the expressions we find that they are suggestive rather than clearcut and precise. Let us start with the Pauline passage which raises and addresses itself to the questions, 'How are the dead raised? In what kind of body?' (*I Corinthians* 15:35). Paul is perturbed at the foolishness of the question, he says. But what is the reason for that? Why should he be? It is the most logical question to ask, if one has been invited to believe in a resurrection from the dead. For the dead either will have a body or will not have a body. If they have a body it will be either a new body or the old body changed. What surprised Paul was the doubt which the questions express. He was himself quite sure that the resurrection was bodily, and surprised that this should be called into question. He attempts in the answer he gives to these questions' (vv. 36-57), to provide illustrations and expositions which will appeal to his readers and convince them to believe as he does that resurrection involves bodiliness.

Paul produces a series of illustrations and arguments to establish the conclusion for his readers. We shall briefly summarise the line he takes. (1) The earthly body is like a bare kernel of wheat which comes to life in a new form only after it has died (vv. 37, 38). (2) There are different kinds of bodies: of men, of beasts, of birds and of fish, so why should there not be another kind, a resurrection body, with a 'splendour' different from the earthly body, as the 'splendour' of one star differs from that of another? What is 'sown as an animal body ... is raised as a spiritual body' (v. 43). (3) The first Adam was of the dust, possessing an animal body. The last Adam 'has become a life-giving Spirit' (v. 45). This explicit contrast between Adam, man who died, and Jesus Christ, man who conquered death, asserts that the ground of the resurrection hope is in Jesus Christ. It also asserts a direct relationship between the resurrected believer and the resurrected Christ. *He* was 'from heaven': so *we* shall wear the likeness of the heavenly man' (vv. 47, 49). (4) While therefore 'flesh and blood can never possess the kingdom of God, and the perishable cannot possess immortality' (v. 50), the fact that we shall not retain this identical bodily form does not mean that the resurrection is to be bodiless existence. 'We shall all be changed' (v. 51). The perishable will be clothed with imperishable, the mortal clothed with immortality.

4 THE DEATH OF JESUS AND THE DEATH OF THE BELIEVER

It is clear that the early Christians associated the death of Jesus with the death of the believer. Jesus had risen from the dead. So there was hope for the believer. Moreover, since from the beginning, the apostolic church expected the Second Coming of Jesus, they believed that it would be a very short time before they would receive their reward. This meant for them that the victory of Jesus over death could be translated into a concrete hope they expected to be fulfilled immediately. The effect of Jesus' 'work' takes in the death of the believer. Jesus died and rose again. There were several implications for the early Christians.

First, some of them thought that since Jesus had conquered death, the believer would not now die. It was a matter of waiting for the immediate return of Jesus, when all believers would be translated. There is evidence that when, in due course, some believers died, something of a crisis occurred. Had they misunderstood the preaching of Paul about the effectiveness of the work of Jesus Christ? Had they been misled about the Second Advent? Was Paul wrong? Was the Christian message, therefore, one big mistake? Were those who had died now at a distinct disadvantage, assuming that the Advent would duly and shortly take place? Such were the questions the death of members of the congregation raised.

So Paul wrote to the newly-emerged group of Christians in the European town of Thessalonica: 'For we would not have you ignorant, brethren, concerning those who are asleep, that you may not grieve as others who have no hope' (*I Thessalonians* 4:13). A double adjustment took place in their thinking. So as to maintain the conquest of death by Jesus, Paul made two proposals: first, the living had no privilege, or — which is the same — the dead were at no disadvantage. The living and the dead were on a par; and second, this equality would be made manifest at the *parousia*, when the living and the dead would meet and 'be with' the Lord together (vv. 15-17). So there was reason for mutual comfort (v. 18). The separation which death brought was not final. So in view of his impending death, the believer could be assured in his hope. Jesus had conquered death. Jesus would in due course display this victory. The believer would share in it at the last day. Those who had died in faith and those who still lived were both included. There would be no difference between them.

Jesus' death and resurrection was the means through which death would be overcome. This belief was an important strand in early Christian theology. It was not always a dominant theme, although in the Eastern Church's theology it was more prominent than in the West. Athanasius, who lived from about AD 295 to 373, argued that the proof that death had been conquered by the cross was to be found in the way in which the Christian had no fear of death, since he knew that there was life beyond it. He wrote, 'But now that the Saviour has raised his body, death is no longer terrible, but all those who believe in Christ tread it underfoot as nothing, and prefer to die, rather than to deny their faith in Christ, knowing full well that when they die they do not perish, but live indeed, and become incorruptible through the resurrection.'[7]

A theology of sin was connected with a theology of death and the idea of resurrection was used in both contexts. Jesus had conquered sin *and* death through his death and resurrection. Sin and death were related as cause to effect, as act to penalty, so that

---

7 Athanasius, *On The Incarnation*, 27.

to overcome sin was to overcome death, and the overcoming of death meant the overthrowing of sin. So analogies are drawn from death and resurrection to faith. Passing from unfaith to faith was like passing from death to life. The relation of the believer to sin was like the relation of the believer to death. He shared in Jesus' resurrection victory. Believing that death had been overcome — had not Jesus been raised from the dead? — he believed that sin would also be overcome. The ease with which Paul can move from the one to the other is quite astonishing, as he does, for example, in the statement in *Romans* chapter six: 'But if we have died with Christ, we believe that we shall also live with him. For we know that Christ being raised from the dead will never die again; death no longer has dominion over him. The death he died he died to sin, once for all, but the life he lives he lives to God. So you also must consider yourselves dead to sin and alive to God in Christ Jesus. Let not sin therefore reign in your mortal bodies' (*Romans* 6:8-12).

In the Western Church and in particular in conservative Protestantism, the victory over death is assumed. God in Jesus Christ has overcome death. So what the believer must do is to ensure that he overcomes sin (of course, by the grace of God), for in doing so he will share in the fruits of Jesus' vanquishing of death. By and large, believers hope that they will do so. One hardly talks enthusiastically about heaven if one really expects to end up in hell. Those who believe that they share in the goodness of God now are those who believe that they will share it in the life to come, however inadequately their theology expresses this hope.

The third implication for the believer of the assertion that Jesus died and rose again is that, in faith in Jesus one need not fear death, that is to say, the experience of dying. Those who live in faith may die in hope. Death has no terror, no sting. In anticipation of the resurrection, one may even now say, 'Death is swallowed up in victory. O death, where is thy victory? O death, Where is thy sting?' (*I Corinthians* 15:54, 55). The revelation of God in the midst of human life enables the believer to face death with courage and

Death, Immortality, and Resurrection

with purpose, with hopeful resignation, with the sense of safety and security in his faith that God is good.

But what does it mean that death is overcome if we still continue to die? Surely it is a hollow victory if what is said to have been overcome still continues as it ever did! How can one say, as Paul does, 'Thanks be to God,' if death still claims us all? The victory cannot be that death no longer has its universal claim, but that in face of the universal reality of death something decisive has taken place. That can only mean that the effect of the dying of Jesus upon death will make itself manifest only after death. The case rests upon what happens after death. Since death has been vanquished, the attitude of the believer in this life, which he knows will end in death, is one of hope. What he believes will happen after death, when the results of Jesus' death and resurrection will manifest themselves, makes a difference to his life before death. How?

Death no longer means despair, emptiness and frustrated hope, for what is to follow is fulfilment. The vanquishing of death is the assurance, that for the believer, and so for the human reality, there is personal existence after death. The intervention of death to close off human consciousness does not mark the extinction of human reality.

5 Jesus' resurrection and believers' resurrection

The New Testament connects the question about the nature of the resurrection life with its teaching about the resurrection of Jesus Christ. 'If there is to be a resurrection, what is the resurrection life going to be like?' would seem to be a natural question to ask. It had already been asked by the New Testament writers themselves. The facts about Jesus the earliest believers accepted were (1) that Jesus had risen from the dead and (2) that he was then possessed of a body, although they find some difficulty in conveying their impressions about it, or even finding categories in which to speak of it.

On the basis of their belief in the resurrection of Jesus, they then proceed to speak of the resurrection of the dead. Jesus had risen from the dead and had appeared in bodily form. Is there some connection between the resurrection body of Jesus and the resurrection body of believers? If the body of believers is to be like the body of the resurrected Christ, and if it is difficult to speak of the appearances of the risen Christ are we not compounding difficulties by setting the two side by side? Paul believed that it was helpful to do so, even if he found that he could only speak with some hesitation about the resurrected Christ.

The body of Jesus is a glorified body. The resurrection body of believers will be like that of Jesus: 'We await a Saviour, the Lord Jesus Christ, who will change our lowly body to be like his glorious body' (*Philippians* 3:21). Note the contrast between 'lowly body,' and 'glorious body.'

So Paul drew a distinction between the body which dies and the body which is raised. The first he calls a physical body (*soma psuchikon*), the second a spiritual body (*soma pneumatikon*). This contrast comes at the end of a series of other contrasts which he makes as he tries to show both that the resurrection body is real, and that it is different from the body which we have. 'So is it with the resurrection of the dead. What is sown is perishable, what is raised is imperishable. It is sown in dishonour, it is raised in glory. It is sown in weakness, it is raised is power. It is sown a physical body, it is raised a spiritual body' (*I Corinthians* 15:42-44).

Paul draws a further contrast between 'the first man Adam' and 'the last Adam' in the ensuing verse. He has thought deeply about the traditions of the resurrected Christ which he had received' (v. 3), and of the appearance of the resurrected Christ to himself (v. 8). The contrast which he draws between the 'earthly' body and the 'heavenly' (vv. 47-48), is based upon his convictions concerning the resurrected Christ. Paul believed Christ to be representative man.

So he writes, 'by a man also came ... the resurrection of the dead' (v. 21). The contrast between Adam and Jesus, both of whom are representative figures, Adam summing up in himself the sinfulness of man, and Jesus opening up for man the possibilities of a new life, became a familiar theme in Christian theology. Jesus goes over the

Death, Immortality, and Resurrection

ground Adam went over, but with the opposite results. So, since Jesus is representative man, he can undo the results of Adam's sin, and give him a new start.[8]

The passages quoted suffice to illustrate Paul's line of thought. It moves from his encounter with the risen Christ, to the traditions about the resurrection handed down to him about the body of the risen Christ and about the appearances, to the certainty of a future resurrection of believers. He finds that future life quite inconceivable except in terms of a body, a body like that of the resurrected Christ.

It will be instructive, therefore, to look briefly at how the Bible thinks about the body.

The Hebrew thought of man as a living body, not as a soul in a body. H. Wheeler Robinson wrote, 'The Hebrew psychology, on the other hand (that is to say, in contrast to Plato), started not with an indwelling soul, but with an animated body, each of its physical members having psychical and ethical qualities.' 'In the Hebrew conception, the body, not the soul, is the essential personality as the body is indeed animated by the soul, in each of its members, but then each of these, by a sort of diffused consciousness, shares in the psychical and ethical, as well as the physical, life of the body.'[9]

The nature of life after the resurrection is for the Hebrew, Paul, determined by this understanding of man. It was quite inconceivable for him that there should be no bodily existence. The very thought of any kind of existence, any kind of consciousness which would be continuous with this one, was intrinsically bound with

---

8 Irenaeus, ca. AD 130 - ca. AD 202, works out the contrast in his fascinating teaching of recapitulation, or *anakephaleiosis*. As Adam was representative of sinful man, so Christ as second Adam is representative of man, and gives man the opportunity which he lost in Eden, since the 'second man' goes over the ground again with different results. Irenaeus makes a detailed comparison between Adam and Christ in his work *Against Heresies*. For a sample see C.C. Richardson (editor) *Early Christian Fathers*. Philadelphia: Westminster Press, 1952. pp. 389-391.

9 H. Wheeler Robinson, *Corporate Personality in Ancient Israel*. Philadelphia: Fortress. Press, 1964. pp. 22,33. Cf. p. 6.

the body. Human existence was bodily existence. There could be no human existence without a body. That was impossible. So if the resurrection body were not identical with this one, then it would be of a different order, an order suited to the world in which it would exist. But there could be no bodiless consciousness.

So we return to the resurrection state of Jesus, according to the earliest records. That Jesus rose in the body is taught in *Luke* 24:39-43 where he appears to his disciples. They react in great fear and terror, because they think that it is a spirit. It was an inconceivable and terrifying thought that the risen Jesus was a ghost (*pneuma*). It is rejected out of hand. 'The notion of a disembodied person is repugnant to the Hebrew mind; a *pneuma* is something unnatural, monstrous, and evil, and the idea that the Risen Christ is such a *pneuma* is rejected with horror.'[10]

Jesus assures them of the reality of his body by inviting them to touch him, hands and feet, and by eating in front of them. Similarly, Jesus convinces Thomas of the reality of his body, and so of the fact of his resurrection, by inviting him to touch him (*John* 20:26-29).

But there were strange features about this body. That is clear from the accounts of the resurrection appearances and disappearances. All to whom he appeared came to believe in him. There are no records of appearances to unbelievers. Even the five hundred of whom Paul heard are called 'brethren' (*adelphoi*), a word reserved for members of the Christian fellowship. So the appearances are faith-creating occasions, witnessed to by those who came to believe, and written down by believers. The appearances ceased after a short period of 'forty days' and then the preaching began. Jesus was exalted. He has begun a new activity and has entered upon a new mode of existence. It was during this period between Passover and Pentecost that Christian faith arose. Put simply: after the death of Jesus, they came to believe in him as the Christ. Hope sprang

---

10 Alan Richardson, *An Introduction to the Theology of the New Testament*. London: S.C.M. Press, 1958. p. 196.

Death, Immortality, and Resurrection

from faith, a hope which moved beyond death and which gave rise to confidence that the enemy, death, had been overcome.

6 THE METAPHOR OF SLEEP

The metaphor of sleep is, in the New Testament, sometimes used of death, and the state of being dead. Awaking thus becomes a figure of the resurrection. To sleep is to be in a condition of hope that one will be awakened. So when the term 'to sleep' (*katheudo*) is used, it implies the suggestion of hope. He who sleeps will wake. He who dies will arise to new life. To those who have faith in Jesus Christ there is the hopeful expectation that after the period that passes following death, there will be the moment of renewal, the awakening of resurrection, and fruitful participation in the life beyond it. Jesus has become 'the first fruits of them that sleep' (*I Corinthians* 15:20). He anticipates the future renewal through his resurrection from the dead. The first cut sheaf presented before Yahweh represents the expectation of the harvest to come. The bounty of a forthcoming crop is anticipated in ceremony. 'On the day of the first fruits, when you offer a cereal offering, of new grain to the LORD at your feast of weeks, you shall have an holy convocation: you shall do no laborious work' (*Numbers* 28:26). So also the restoration of new life is anticipated in the resurrection of Jesus Christ.

So, in view of this anticipation, death can be called 'sleep.' Paul speaks of 'those who are asleep,' 'those who have fallen asleep,' in explicit contrast to 'we who are alive.' (*I Thessalonians* 4:13-15, 17). He speaks of them as subjects of hope. They who are dead are to be considered subjects of God's gracious gift of life equally with those who are alive. The gift is in Jesus Christ 'who died for us so that whether we wake or sleep we might live with him' (*I Thessalonians* 5:10).

This same use of 'sleep,' referring to a state of death in which there is hope of living again we have seen in these Pauline passages, is also found in the Gospels. In two instances where Jesus confronts the dead, he speaks of death as a sleep, and in neither case do his hearers understand the significance of the metaphor. 'Lazarus is dead,' but Jesus says that he has 'fallen asleep,' and Jesus will wake him from his sleep (*John* 11:11-14). The young girl at the house of Jairus is dead, and already the hired mourners are wailing and shrieking. But they literally change their tune and laugh when they hear Jesus say, 'The child is not dead but sleeping' (*Mark* 5:39, 40). Luke adds the reason for the mourners' laughter: 'And they laughed at him, knowing that she was dead' (*Luke* 8:53). Paid mourners do not wail for people who merely sleep. That is laughable. They missed the meaning of the metaphor. The irony of the situation was that they did not need to mourn, as if there were no hope. So where there is Christian faith, there is hope.

The term 'sleep' is used of one who has died but will live again. Death is not the end. There is an end to the interim which death brings. The use of the metaphor of sleep suggests hope. To die with hope of resurrection is to sleep. If a person sleeps, he wakes to new life when the sleep is done. So the Hebrew with his earlier belief in *Sheol*, 'the pit,' 'the place of the shades,' had room, in the end, for the metaphor of sleep. Later writers speak of an awakening, and believe that after the awakening there comes reward and punishment. Here in the Old Testament, in a later writing, there is an explicit co-ordination of 'awakening' and 'everlasting life.' The passage in view reads as follows: 'And many of those who sleep in the dust of the earth shall awake, some to everlasting life, and some to shame and everlasting contempt.' (*Daniel* 12:2). We have noticed an advance on this idea in the teaching of the Epistles and the Gospels, where the sleep of death is viewed from the point of view of Christian faith.

For those whose relation to God is shaped by their faith in Jesus Christ, death is not the end. That relationship continues beyond death. Resurrection and eternal life are, in the New Testament, always related to what God has done in Jesus Christ. The relationship of faith with Jesus Christ makes such hope possible.

Death, Immortality, and Resurrection

Some interesting issues are raised by this evidence. We may note, in passing, that (to quote John Calvin) 'nowhere in Scripture is the term "sleep" applied to the soul when it is used to designate death.'[11] We need not pause now to discuss this point further, since we shall shortly ask, What is the proper subject of immortality?

To apply the idea of sleep to death leads to a question concerning the post-mortem state, or states. Sleep is a period when consciousness is not 'full.' The beginning of sleep marks the end of one period. The end of sleep marks the beginning of another. So sleep represents the transition from an old state to a new beginning, a transition to new opportunity. Since it is normal to sleep at night, the passage from darkness to light is parallel to the passage from the state of sleep to the state of wakefulness, from weariness and exhaustion to that of freshness and energy. Repose heals. One wakes feeling renewed and refreshed.

Once again we notice a double application of the symbol of sleep, of darkness and light: now to death, and now to the transition from the old life to the new.

As used of death the figure of sleep points us then to three states: this life, an interim state and a final state. It raises the question of the interim state, the second state, and is here that it becomes somewhat ambiguous. Sleep is a form of consciousness and, as we all know, there are levels of sleep, deep sleep, light sleep. But even if we are asleep we still respond to stimuli. How could someone or something awake us if we did not respond in the state of sleep? But still we do not call sleep itself a state of consciousness. Moreover, dreams take place while we sleep. We experience in our dreams a quite different form of consciousness from what we do when we are awake. Here there takes place a non-logical co-ordination of images. We 'know' ourselves to be involved in what is happening. We 'experience' fear and ecstasy, for example. But, in the dreaming state, we are not as we are when we are awake. Hence the inverted commas. We can hardly say that the events of our dreams are comparable to the events of our waking life. We feel that we have to put

---

11 John Calvin, *Tracts and Treatises*. Michigan: Eerdmans, Volume III, p. 459.

inverted commas around such terms as 'happening,' 'event' when we use them of sleep. We would not speak, for example, about making decisions in our dreams. To speak of death as sleep raises the question whether, if there is an interim state, it is something like that state of dreaming. This, you will remember, was Hamlet's question, as he reflected on the problem of what lay beyond death. He contemplated the possibility that after this life there might be unknown and unwelcome dreams:

> ....To die, to sleep.
> To sleep, perchance to dream. Ay there's the rub,
> For in that sleep of death what dreams may come
> When we have shuffled off this mortal coil
> Must give us pause.[12]

The possibility of bad dreams made him and has made many another, hesitate and tremble at the thought of death, at the thought of the prospect of self-inflicted death. And if we do not have our own visions of the possibility of bad dreams, others may provide them for us, as for example in the preaching of hell fire.

So the figure of sleep makes various suggestions not altogether congenial to the theist's beliefs. When we ask, 'What is the nature of the post-mortem state?' and 'What is the relation of that state to this life?' there are two unknowns. The figure of sleep suggests the analogy that death is to life as sleep is to waking. But, if we do not wish to be confused, we had better take 'sleep' as a simile and say that we are indicating in a somewhat poetic way some meanings rather than others. So we make qualifications for example: Death is like a *dreamless* sleep. One is not conscious when one is dead. But there is an end to the unconsciousness introduced at death. This end takes place at the resurrection. That is like waking up after sleep, like the renewal of consciousness, after a period of unknowing.

To introduce the fact of dreaming is perhaps not relevant in this context. For we can take the notion of sleep and subtract from

---

12 *Hamlet*, Act 3, Scene 1, ll. 66-70.

Death, Immortality, and Resurrection

it the fact of dreaming. Then we have dreamless sleep. That would harmonise with the Hebrew notion of *sheol*. Taken in this way, the analogy of sleep suggests subtraction of consciousness at death, and waking from sleep suggests the renewal of consciousness at the resurrection.

The New Testament usage of the figure is quite clear. To use the term 'sleep' of death, and 'sleeping' of the dead, is to indicate that death will not be the final end of conscious life. It is to claim that if there is to be a renewal of conscious life there must be a resurrection; that, since this takes place on the initiative of the gracious God who raised up Jesus from the dead, the Christian believer may have hope, and need not sorrow as those who have no hope.

7 The interim state

But what of the interim state?

By the expression 'the interim state' we mean the state between death and the end. Oscar Cullmann, in a significant but short book,[13] insists that we must consider this period and read it in the light of the Christian faith. Since the transformation of the body does not take place until the end, a literal temporal end, this raises the question of 'the interim condition' of the dead' (78). Christ has conquered death and brought life and incorruptibility to light' (II *Timothy* 1:10), but while death has been conquered, 'it will not be abolished until the end.' The last enemy to be destroyed is death, when 'death will be no more' (*Revelation* 21:4).

Yet believers still die, even as they did following the resurrection of Jesus. However, the resurrection age has been inaugurated. It awaits its consummation. So, for the believer, who shares in the conquest of death, death has lost its terror. The tension between 'already fulfilled' and 'not yet consummated' belongs to the fabric of the New Testament, according to Cullmann (75). Since Easter is

---

13 Oscar Cullmann, *Immortality of the Soul or Resurrection of the Dead? The Witness of the New Testament*. Reprinted in Terence Penelhum (ed.), *Immortality*. Belmont, California: Wandsworth Publishing Company, Inc., 1973. pp. 53-85. References in the text are to this work.

the starting-point of the existence, life and thought of the Christian church, we are living in an interim time. 'The decisive battle has been fought in Christ's death and resurrection; only V-day is yet to come' (75). The end-time is already present but there is a 'temporal interval' which separates Jesus' resurrection from our own. The foretaste of the consummation is given through the Holy Spirit, who manifests himself in the breaking of the bread, the 'communion with the body of Christ' (*I Corinthians* 10:16).

Death will be abolished at the end. It has already been conquered. So there is an interim period between the conquest and the annihilation of death. This means that the dead are still in some way 'in time,' since the resurrection, according to Cullmann, takes place at a point in time. The dead are not in their interim condition placed beyond time. For Cullmann, this means that they are not immortal, since immortality would mean loosing the bounds of time and that would make resurrection superfluous. The transformation of the body does not, indeed cannot, take place at death, since the victory over death at the End is a cosmic event.

There is no New Testament evidence for the view that the resurrection of the body takes place immediately after the death of the individual (79).[14] To be 'with Christ,' 'in paradise,' 'in Abraham's bosom,' 'under the altar,' are images to express 'special nearness to God' (80). The usual way Paul expresses it when he speaks of the dead is that they are asleep. He believes that there was a difference between the state of the Christian in death, and the one who had not believed. Cullmann says they are 'closer to the final resurrection,' 'no longer alone,' but does not go in for any extensive description about their condition. They are 'with the Lord.' All these expressions are attempts to express the conviction that the believer may have hope. But can we be more specific? The dead wait. They sleep. But how? He denies that the state of the dead is that state indicated by the phrase 'immortality of the soul.' He distinguishes the condition of the believer after death from the con-

---

14 Cullmann refers to such passages as *I Thessalonians 4:13ff.*, *Revelation 6:11*, *Luke* 23:43, 16:22, *Philippians* 1:23 in making this denial.

Death, Immortality, and Resurrection

dition of one who does not share in the fruits of Jesus' victory over death. So Cullmann says, even in this state they are already 'living with Christ' (83). They may even have a certain consciousness. So he claims: '*we* wait, and *the dead* wait. Of course the rhythm of time may be different for them than for the living; and in this way the interim time may be foreshortened for them .... (T)his expression *to sleep* which is the customary designation in the New Testament of the 'interim condition,' draws us to the view that for the dead another time-consciousness exists, that of 'those who sleep.'

But that does not mean that the dead are not still in time. '.... (T)he New Testament resurrection hope is different from the Greek belief in immortality' (84). Cullmann is relying upon a certain interpretation of the imagery of sleep to make good his position about the interim state. So we ask, How is this imagery of sleep to be taken? In our previous discussion, we pointed out that it has limited application. It suggests a range of ideas. But not all of these are relevant to theological discussion of death. It is a question of how the limits are to be set. Cullmann moves rather tentatively from the figure of sleep to the conclusion that in death for the believer there is some kind of consciousness in time, albeit a different kind of time from the ones we now know. But why, in applying the analogy of sleep to death should we take it to imply consciousness at all?

The idea of sleep suggests *contrast, transition, continuity*. Thus it offers hope. We can certainly retain these ideas concerning death without speaking of survival on some level of consciousness in the interim period following death. We may retain Cullmann's ideas (1) of an interim state, (2) of a difference between the believing and the unbelieving dead, (3) that there is an objective ground for the hope that differentiates those who die in Jesus Christ, namely the God whom Jesus Christ reveals. We need not, and shall not then speculate fruitlessly about the condition of the interim state.

We, the living, who bear witness to the fact that God 'is not the God of the dead but of the living' (*Mark* 12:27), speak of the dead with hope. That hope is in the living God, who has made himself known in Jesus Christ.

If there is to be a life hereafter and if the soul is not immortal, then death introduces an interim state between one existence and another.

We are denying (1) that the soul is inherently immortal, (2) that the soul (defined as one element in a dualistic being) sleeps. (3) that there is conscious life at death. The state is 'interim' in being between one state of being which is past and gone for ever, and another which can be anticipated. There is hope of further life beyond death.

Time is a problem for Cullmann. We need a much more extensive discussion to do the concept justice. Time is a form of human existence. It is a structure we impose to make sense of our experiences. Time is thus a condition of being able to experience anything at all. To predicate time of the human creature is to predicate consciousness. So for the conscious the body of the dead is in the grave and there is a date on the gravestone. Meanwhile we live our lives in time.

So why not rather simply speak of death as the end of consciousness, the person ceasing to exist, and then speak of restoration of consciousness continuous with the earthly consciousness, or related in a specific way at the resurrection to such consciousness? We may then be able to answer more clearly the important question, 'What is the proper subject of immortality?

8 Concrete social relationships

The concern of the biblical writers is with the concrete human being in quite particular relationships with his fellow, with man incorporate, or as we now say, social relationships.

We become human by being in relationship with other human beings. There is no isolation of man from his fellows in the Bible. One is constituted as a person by one's social relationships. There is no thought of man apart from one's society. One's very being is in relationship with one's community, a relationship which sustains one throughout one's life, and which endures through time, as long as the community lasts. The Hebrew moved easily from the individual to the group and from the group to the individual. 'Human personality is in itself as truly social as individual.'

Yahweh is the God of *the people* Israel, the nation as a whole. So man is in solidarity with his fellows who are in covenant with God. The members of the people are of one blood with the ancestors and with one another. They share in the consequences of the fathers' deeds. They become involved in the sins of the fathers. In the sin of one man, Achan for example, the whole people is thought of as sinning and so the sin must be purged from the midst of the people. We cannot pursue this most interesting topic further here.[15]

These biblical perspectives are important for our reflections about life after death. Even if the biblical writers did not themselves always draw conclusions about life after death from their convictions, it is reasonable to hold that if there is life after death in any sense in continuity with this life, such post-mortem life will be social. It is in harmony with the Hebrew conviction that life after death be life in relation, that it be then as now constituted by relationships.

Moreover, for biblical writers, man is a unity, an integrated person, not an animated body, or an enfleshed spirit. Man is not a soul housed in a body. Man *is* soul. Suffice it to say that the biblical writers know of no dichotomies or trichotomies.

The proper subject of religion is the human being (1) as a psycho-somatic unity, and (2) as a social creature shaped by being in relationships with community, tribe, family, nation. We who are shaped by our relations with our fellows are, through these ties, able to comprehend and to express the revelation of God. We are historical beings. It is as such creatures that we are the subjects of God's care, and as such the ones who receive the benefit of the revelation

---

15 A classical treatment of this subject is in H. Wheeler Robinson, *Corporate Personality in Ancient Israel*. Philadelphia: Fortress Press, 1964. The quotation is from p. 21.

of God. Then, that is to say, after God has revealed himself to man, man now stands under and in the love of God. God is known to us as human beings, as we are in relationships with one another.

We as historical beings, are *constituted* by being in dialog with our fellows. To be in relation is to become human. God is known in the midst of human community. Man's co-humanity points beyond itself to God, the transcendent.[16]

It would be strange if it would be otherwise with life after death. The proper subject of immortality is the human creature, the person in the concreteness of relationships with other persons. So human life in its concrete fulfilment is to be the model of what immortal life will be. So say the biblical writers. They insist that the human creature is a unity of many facets, is a creature constituted by relationship.

When we speak of man in concrete relationships as the proper subject of immortality we are not relying upon those hints of the nature of the afterlife and of the state of man in death to be found in the Bible. Nor are we relying upon the meaning of certain terms used in the Bible. The tenor of the Biblical view is to deny an innate immortality to men, to affirm a state of unconsciousness in death and to affirm also that God bestows the gift of eternal life to the person, after death according as he wills. This is representative of the biblical evidence. It is also a rationally defensible position.

9 Person — THE UNITY OF A LIVING BEING

The Bible teaches that man is a unity. The Hebrew term for soul, *nephesh*, does not refer to an element independent of the body, the real man, possessing immortality in its own right. The word *nephesh* means personality, individuality, vitality. It is quite impossible that soul should exist independent of the body. This is

---

16 Ronald G. Smith spoke of man being known in the 'interstices of human relationships.' Drawing on Martin Buber, he taught that the experience of 'the other,' that is our fellow human beings, is the very thing that enables us to be human. Cf. *The Doctrine of God*. Philadelphia: The Westminster Press, 1970. pp. 128-143.

Death, Immortality, and Resurrection

evident in the Old Testament use of the word *nephesh*, and in the New Testament use of *psuche*.

The term *nephesh* is used over seven hundred and fifty times in the Old Testament. There is no exact equivalent in English, a fact which explains why the translators of the King James Version used over forty different English words to translate it as it occurred in different contexts. In none of its uses is there any suggestion of inherent, natural immortality.

Only when God creates him does man become a living *nephesh*: 'Then the LORD God formed man of dust from the ground, and breathed into his nostrils the breath of life; and man became a living *being*' (*Genesis* 2:7). The term is used to signify 'life' (as in *Exodus* 4:19, *Deuteronomy* 19:21 and *I Samuel* 19:11) as opposed to death. It is used as equivalent to 'a man' and in the plural as equivalent to 'persons,' 'people.' 'All the persons of the house of Jacob were seventy' (*Genesis* 46:27, cf. 12:5). The word *nephesh* could even be used of the dead, as in the prohibition: 'You shall not make any cuttings in your flesh on account of the dead' (*Leviticus* 19:28); 'He shall not go near a dead body' (*Numbers* 6:6). The term *nephesh*, sometimes rendered 'soul', here means a corpse.

There are three chief uses of the term *nephesh*.[17] (1) It means life as opposed to death. (2) It is used where we would speak of a person, a human being, and its plural where we would say 'people.' (3) It is the *nephesh* that experiences everything, whether it belongs to the realm of feeling, of knowing or of willing.

Soul, *nephesh*, is the breath, the principle of life, the centre of consciousness, and then by extension, the inner consciousness of life. The breath is life. Breathing we live. Without breath we die. The Hebrew thought of breath as giving life to all parts of the body. Life was restored to the dead child when Elijah prayed. He prayed that the child's *nephesh* be given again to him. 'O LORD my God, let this child's *soul* come into him again.' Life was restored to the

---

17 Cf. G. Ryder Smith, *The Bible Doctrine of Man*. London: The Epworth Press, 1951, pp. 6-9.

widow of Zarephath's son when Elijah prayed.' The child' s *nephesh* returned upon his inward parts and he lived' (*I Kings* 17:22).[18]

Similarly, the New Testament uses *psuche* of life, of the person. The disciple is to take no thought for his *psuche* (*Matthew* 6:23). The *life* of the young Eutychus, thought to have been dead, is still in him (*Acts* 20:10). We can compare the word *psuche* to the word *nephesh*. Like the Hebrew word, the Greek word can stand for the breath, the breath of life, the personal and reflexive pronouns, e.g. I, she, myself, herself, the seat of the personality, the person. So it can mean a human being as a psycho-somatic unity. The soul, *psuche*, can be gained or lost. So a person is to act with due care. 'For whoever would save his *life* will lose it; and whoever loses his *life* for my sake and the gospel's will save it. For what does it profit a man to gain the whole world and forfeit his life?' (*Mark* 8:35-37). Jesus illustrated this unselfish, un-hedonistic way of thinking, for 'he gave his *psuche* for many' (*Matthew* 20:28).

The adjective from *psuche*, namely *psuchikos*, is rather derogatory, since it contrasts with *pneumatikos* meaning 'spiritual.' The word appears in this contrasting sense at *I Corinthians* 15:44,46 whereas it is rendered 'physical' in contrast to 'spiritual.' Paul is drawing a contrast between the body which dies and the body of the resurrection. The present body is physical, *psuchikos*, whereas the resurrection body is *pneumatikos*, spiritual. It is sown a 'physical body, it is raised a spiritual body ... but it is not the spiritual which is first but the physical, and then the spiritual.' Adam is a man of mere soul, not spirit. The 'psychic' stands in contrast to the spiritual man. He, the former, is 'natural' (K.J.V). Nothing could more clearly indicate human non-immortality. Man is mortal. Paul quotes *Genesis* 2:7 in *I Corinthians* 15:45 and uses the term *psuche* for the Hebrew *nephesh*. And so it is written, 'The first man Adam was made a living soul; the last Adam was made a quickening spirit.' A living 'soul' means a living being, a live animate person. Note the

---

18 The translation is by H. Wheeler Robinson, *Religious Ideas of the Old Testament*. London: Duckworth, 1964. p. 80.

Death, Immortality, and Resurrection

following brief summary of the Pauline use of the term *psuche*.[19] 'Just as Paul does not know the Greek-Hellenistic conception of the immortality of the soul (released from the body), neither does he use *psuche* to designate the seat or the power of the mental life which animates man's matter, as it had become the custom to do among the Greeks. Rather *psuche* in Paul means primarily the Old Testament *nephesh* (rendered *psuche* in the LXX) — 'vitality' or 'life' itself.... Where the contrast with *pneuma* is not involved, Paul uses *psuche* altogether in the sense current in the Old Testament-Jewish tradition; viz. to designate human life, or rather to denote man as a living being .... *psuche* is that specifically human state of being alive which inheres in man as a striving, willing, purposing self ... full human life .... the natural life of earthly man, of course, in contrast to supranatural life.'

10 THE PROPER SUBJECT OF IMMORTALITY?

We now have our answer to the question, 'What is the proper subject of immortality?' It is the human being, the person, the subject of both Old and New Testaments.

11 ETERNAL LIFE

'Eternal life' accompanies belief in Jesus Christ, and has its initial source in the love of God. 'Everyone who has faith in him may not die but (may) have eternal life.' Those who have faith in Jesus, the Son of Man,' may in him possess eternal life' (*John* 3:15, 16 NEB). The believer, as it were, drinks from a spring of living and life-giving water which produces eternal life. This has its source in Jesus (4:14). To hear obediently and to respond to the word of Scripture, and not simply to learn the letter, is to receive eternal life (5:24, 39). God's word is a word of commandment. The disciple, like Jesus himself, responds in happy obedience to this commandment and such a life of willing response is 'eternal

---

19 Rudolf Bultmann, *Theology of the New Testament*. Vol. l. Translated by Kendrick Grobel. London: S.C.M. Press, 1956. pp. 203-205.

life' (12:50). Eternal life is a life of responsiveness to God and in relation to him. Jesus speaks the words of eternal life (6:68). The *words* of Jesus are the source of eternal life to those who hear and believe. To believe is to have eternal life: 'Truly, truly, I say to you, he who believes has eternal life' (6:47, 40). Jesus' words are like the food and drink which sustain eternal life (6:27, 55, 56). Eternal life is a gift: 'I give them eternal life'(10:28). The disciple is prepared to abandon his soul (= life), his *psuche*. That he can readily do, for he has already received eternal life which cannot he taken from him (12:25). When the work of Jesus is complete, he will have eternal life as God's gift. Eternal life is to 'know God.' 'This is eternal life: to know thee who alone art truly God and Jesus Christ whom thou hast sent' (17:2, 3 NEB).

III Immortality and Other Words

1 We value human life

Many Christians, perhaps most Christians in the past, have taken immortality for granted. They have been encouraged to do so both by church teachers, by theologians and by philosophers. We all have a desire to live on again if the conditions are congenial. The teaching of immortality thus provided an assurance of the truth of a belief which often is pleasing to hold. It looks as if in this case the Christian church has endorsed the wish-fulfilment of human beings. This is such an interesting fact that we must explore the meaning of immortality to see if the hope is well grounded. Before we are able to examine whether we can or cannot reasonably believe in immortality, we must ask what we mean when we speak of it. We shall then be able clearly to say what we do believe and what we do not believe. We can then ask what grounds we have for such belief, examine the writings of the New Testament, and consider the idea of resurrection in relation to that of immortality. We will be interested in particular in the significance of the resurrection of Jesus Christ for the believer.

To speak of mortality is to think of death. To speak of immortality is to think of life. Since death takes place at the end of human life and not at the beginning, we think of what happens after death as the problem, rather than what, if anything, happened before life. We do not see it as a problem that we did not exist before we were born. Why should we then see it as a problem that we may not exist after we have died? For most people what happened, if anything or nothing, before birth is of little concern. My non-existence before birth does not concern me. But the possibility of my non-existence after death does. This reflects, I think, the convictions of many people. Why should existence after life concern me? The answer is that we have tasted human life and have valued it. Sometimes it may have been good, at other times not so good. Where human life has not been good, or not consistently good, where — that is to say — it has not had that interest and value which give it a certain quality, one may at least have become aware of what it might have been. It may be as much the unrealised possibilities of human life that lead us to look hopefully for renewal and continuance, as those possibilities which have been realised.

What we have valued we wish to conserve. We know something of the possibilities of human life, whether we have realised some of them to some extent or whether we have not. If we have found life good we want it to continue. If we have not found life good, we want to have the opportunity to realise what has been denied us. Once having experienced and having valued human life, we believe (perhaps) that any just order of things will preserve what is valuable and good. That, of course, is a great act of faith, but one which explains why *after* having known human life, we find it hard to reconcile ourselves to the possibility of non-existence at death.

2 God bestows immortal life

The meaning of 'immortal' as 'not subject to death' is preserved on condition that whenever such life begins, it does not afterwards cease. Let us consider the possibility that at death a *total* but temporary cessation of human life takes place. Let us suppose that after such a total cessation, human consciousness once more becomes a reality. There was not, and then later there was, such consciousness. Such life would be immortal, provided it did not cease thereafter. Death as the total cessation of the psycho-somatic unity which we call being a person would not stand in contradiction to such immortality, such immortal life. Life that is immortal would then start at a point after human life had ceased at death. The extinction of human consciousness at death does not, therefore, stand in contradiction to immortality. Man dies and ceases to be. After death he may receive immortality.

Such immortality would be conditional immortality. By that we mean that given that death is the end of human consciousness, there would be no further life unless certain conditions sufficient to produce such life after death were to prevail. Christian theology says that such a set of conditions will be operative. It is through that renewal which is the gift and act of God that such life is made possible. It is through resurrection that such immortal life is *bestowed*. It is a gracious gift of God. It is incompatible to speak of the immortality of the soul (in the dualist sense) and the resurrection of the body. Denial of the inevitability of immortality demands a redefinition of the concept of soul.

Belief in immortality as bestowed but not innate is quite harmonious with belief in the 'resurrection of the body' as the New Testament and the Christian teaching express it.

But what sort of life after death can we conceive? Take two polar opposites: greatly enhanced consciousness at the one end of the scale, and greatly diminished consciousness at the other end. There are many levels of consciousness between these. It is only when there is a certain level of consciousness that we may speak of desirable human life.

Mortality means a condition of being prone to die. Immortality means the opposite, namely, a condition of not being prone to die. Mortal man dies. Immortal man does not die. Mortal man is subject to death. Immortal man is not. A being which dies, and so is liable to die, is mortal. A being who does not die, and so is not liable to die, is immortal. The term 'mortal' does not (of course) apply only to *human* being, to *human* life. Similarly it may be the case that there are beings, in contrast to human beings, who are immortal. What we are inquiring is whether we can reasonably apply the term 'immortal' to human life at all. If we can, it will not be exclusive to human life. Immortality means being which is non-liable-to-death, whatever the nature of that being. Of whatever we may say, 'It will not die!' that being is immortal.

The question we then raise is whether such an unqualified idea of immortality can express Christian hope.

Further considerations will make the point clear. The other day I heard of a father whose daughter, a young and very promising adult, intelligent and full of energy, underwent a minor operation. A mistake was made while the anaesthetic was being administered and it caused her irreparable brain damage. She returned home and her father cared for her, or for that shadow of what she once was. There was physical life in the organism which had once expressed her intelligent personality but she that had once been was no more. The pathetic words of the father made the tragedy unforgettable. He said, 'I have lost my girl. She was a great girl.' What he meant was that although she was still alive, such a change had taken place in her that you could not really say it was the same 'she.' She was no longer the same person she had been. Her level of consciousness had been so radically altered, that even although her body, the physical constituents, was virtually identical to what it had been, she was not the same self. She lived on but on a sadly reduced level of consciousness, so reduced that we might even hesitate to call her human.

Changes in consciousness do not necessarily depend upon physical conditions, and they can be of different kinds. We may also speak of an enhanced level of consciousness, where potentialities which had lain dormant are awakened, and one becomes 'more alive,' rather then 'less alive' as in the unhappy case to which we have referred.

Renewal or continuity of consciousness after death would qualify as immortality, provided that it did not cease.

Some kinds of consciousness and some kinds of immortality would not be desirable, or would only be desirable if one could hope that one would move from them, that there would be change to an enhanced level.

Moreover, we talk of life without consciousness and we distinguish between various kinds of life. If immortality means 'life which does not die' it is necessary to clarify what particular kind

Death, Immortality, and Resurrection

of life it is when Christian theists speak of life after death. What Christians have normally insisted is that what they mean is life which is individual, conscious and personal. It is not a question of surviving with the sort of life which we attribute to a plant, a tree, or an animal, but with the sort of life which is at least on no lower level of consciousness than the valued human life which we have known or have known to be possible in this existence.

Other kinds of consciousness would not be desirable. That is basically why the Hindu doctrine of re-incarnation is so pessimistic, so without hope. The soul at death may be re-incarnated into the body of an insect, a beast or a human being. But the process of continued reincarnation could be endless, either upward or downward without progress. The only hope would be to escape from it altogether.

So the bare idea of immortality is of itself of little religious value or interest. It takes on religious import only if the imagination can make it concrete enough. The Christian when speaking about living on after death does not simply mean what the bare concept of immortality suggests. After all 'living on' is a metaphor. In a sense we all live on after we die. We live on in the memories of those who knew us. We live on as what we have done in life continues to have influence. We live on in the mind of God, who remembers what we were. In this sense we do not live literally, and since few human beings achieve much non-literal immortality, few of us live on at all in this way, or if we do it is not for long. According to the statement earlier quoted, however, that is the most that we may hope for — a metaphorical immortality.

The names of earth's greatest will be remembered — that is a certain kind of immortality. But *what* is it that lives on, when we speak in this way? A name, an idea, a dream of what one once was? An historical memory of what one once did, more or less correct, more or less distorted? This is only for the few. The rest of us are remembered in a narrow circle for a while and then forgotten. Those who remember us themselves die. Our light diminishes and finally goes out, for there comes a time when there is none left who remembers us.

> Time like an ever-rolling stream
> Bears all its sons away.
> They fly forgotten as a dream
> Dies at the opening day.[20]

Such a conception of immortality does not express Christian hope. In fact there is nothing Christian about it. We are still left with the question, 'What lives on?' We must continue to look for other ways of qualifying the idea of immortality if it is to express a religious concern.

The idea of immortality has little interest unless what it means can be imagined *concretely*. So when the husband has died, how does the wife imagine him and what does she think relations with him will be like in the resurrection life? When a child has died, how may the mother imagine the possible relation between them after that death? The fact is that the only relationships we know are the relationships we have experienced in this life. So we project such relationships into the next world. Will wife care for husband then? Will mother care for daughter then? What could 'caring' mean then? It has special meaning now because of the family relationships in which human beings are involved. But what could it mean if those family relationships no longer prevail? If, after, death, we no longer have these bodies, if we are 'like the angels in heaven' (to quote the words of the Gospel), who do not marry nor are given in marriage, that is to say who have no sexual and family relations, how can the sort of relations we experience here be meaningfully projected there? Life here is in the body, in the flesh. But if 'flesh and blood shall not inherit the world to come,' how shall we begin to imagine it? And if we cannot imagine it, how can we say that the possibility is a concrete hope? It may be logical possibility. Is it a real one?

---

20 Isaac Watts, *Psalm xc*.

This is an important question. To believe something concretely means that we must have some clear understanding of what it is we are believing. We may not have all the clarity we wish for, but there must be some, and at the crucial points. Even the more agnostic believer has clarity at the crucial point. He may say that he has and needs little idea concerning life after death because he can leave that with God. But he understands that God is good, has some idea what counts for goodness and so believes that the life after death will be good. He believes he knows what good means and believes that God will conserve that goodness in the life he will bestow. He knows himself to be in relationship to a loving God and that suffices him. As he thinks about the matter he finds that certain options are excluded for him, and that he has taken certain decisions about alternative positions.

3 THE FINALITY OF DEATH

Who or what is it that is to be immortal?

There is little doubt who it is that is mortal. One of the first steps you take in learning logic is to see that the syllogism is valid which argues:

All men are mortal.
 Socrates is a man.
Therefore, Socrates is mortal.

Put the name of any man, woman or child in place of Socrates, or include your own. It is valid — the syllogism. The conclusion is true — that you are mortal.

So, are we not faced with a straight contradiction? The Christian says that man is mortal. He also says that he can hope for immortality, or that he is immortal. It is so obvious that we die that it seems contradictory to say that we are — in whatever sense — immortal. It looks like the old trick of playing with words, giving a word, in this case 'mortal' a clear meaning, and then contradicting that meaning. If 'immortal' means 'not subject to death' and we die, it seems contradictory to say of us creatures that die, that we are immortal. Is that not to claim that we die but do not die, that when we die we do not die? Or, that when we die, we do not *really die*? If we put it in that way, we distinguish between 'dying' and 'really dying.' 'Really dying' means that there is an end, oblivion. 'Dying' means that the end is not final. So what sort of an end is death? Make this distinction and you are talking about two different possibilities. The first is that of dying a natural death at the end of an earthly life, but living again afterwards. The second is that of dying a natural death at the end of an earthly life but not living again afterwards.

This distinction can help clarify the meaning of the term 'immortal.' 'Immortal' can mean either that at death consciousness ceases but that it exists again afterwards, or it can mean that consciousness does not cease, even at death. We have seen reason to reject this second alternative.

What emerges from this is that the terms 'mortal' and 'immortal' *can* have the same meaning. We are mortal if we die, but immortal if we live on after death. The term 'mortal' means that one now dies, whether one lives after or not. The term 'immortal' means that one lives for ever after this life, whatever happens at death. One may be both mortal and immortal, mortal in the sense that one dies, immortal in the sense that after death one lives on. They are not simple opposites.

We can now return to our original question, 'What sort of reality is death?' and now can answer, 'Death is final.' To say that man is mortal indicates that finality. To say that man may be immortal indicates that whatever finality death has, it is not the end. Death is the end, but there is life beyond. Death is the end, but it does not have the last word. God does.

4 Immortal life

We must now notice an important meaning of the term 'immortal.' To make this point we shall need to draw some contrasts and comparisons between synonymous words. The two other terms we shall consider are 'eternal' and 'everlasting.' All three words are adjectives and (in the context we are interested to consider) qualify 'life,' as in the phrases, 'eternal life,' 'everlasting life,' 'immortal life.' These different expressions do not have the same meaning.

Everlasting life is life which continues through a temporal series, through an arithmetical infinity of occasions, endless life. The term says nothing about the quality of life, nothing of progress or deterioration. It simply says that life goes on endlessly, without cessation. What lasts persists *through time*. We learn that from our human experience. To speak about life continuing forever throughout time is to project the present experience of temporal passage into the future. Such life will be like the present in moving through time, but with no end. That prospect *could* be frightful, terrifying. Would anyone want life which simply goes on and on and on and on and on .... with no further understanding or guarantee of what *sort* of life it was to be? Would anyone want an infinite extension of this life, howsoever in the limited time he lived, he had enjoyed such life? And if life had been cruel and harsh, would he opt for a never-ending renewal of it in preference to extinction?

Because 'eternal' does not mean the same as 'everlasting', *eternal life* has a different meaning from *everlasting* life. The word 'eternal' lays emphasis on the quality of life and is not a reference simply to the fact of its being without end. 'Eternal' does not primarily have reference to time. There is about some human relationships a certain quality we sometimes describe as timelessness. It is as if time does not matter, does not constitute a barrier or a limitation to, or even a category of, the experience. The believer who stands in relationship to God has such a qualitative relationship with him. The term 'eternal life' designates the quality of such an experience. The term is typically to be found in the Gospel of John. (See the chapter in this book on the teaching of the New Testament).

The believer in God, through Jesus Christ, experiences union with him here and now. He does not have to wait for eternal life until after death. He has it here and now. 'Eternal life' is life which is related to Jesus Christ. What is now experienced is a foretaste of what will be. So the believer is not left in the dark concerning what to expect. The life beyond death will not be radically different from the life experienced in relationship to Jesus Christ, here and now — *eternal* life.

Immortal life is life not subject to death. The term refers to a final state. 'Immortal' means that in the end there will be no mortality, that ultimately there will be being rather than nonbeing. If eternal life is not simply equivalent to life after death, or to everlasting life, immortal life does not simply mean life not subject to death, but rather not subject to *final* death, not subject to *ultimate* extinction. The term does not imply that death is not real. In view of the ambiguity of the term 'immortality' we must make some further observations. Death, we have said, is decisive. It marks the end of earthly, human life. There is no question about the finality of death. The body ceases to function and decays. Its elements are absorbed into the physical world. So we cannot speak of the immortality of the body, or of the immortality of the flesh. We cannot make our immortality depend upon the continuance of the same body, since it is beyond possibility that the identical particles which constituted the body which died shall be reconstituted the same person.

As we have seen, the belief that the actual particles were brought together to reconstitute the resurrection body was called 'the resurrection of the flesh.' This impossible teaching was widely held in the early centuries of Christian thought. It is to be carefully distinguished from belief in the 'resurrection of the body.' Whatever continuity there is between the present life and the future life, it will not be a physical one in the sense that the same constituent parts shall make up the body. That is not even a criterion for identity now. A 'bodily resurrection' does not entail the identity of the particles which made up the body which died.

5 Various alternatives

There are various alternatives open to the Christian who speaks of immortality and seeks to preserve continuity between this life and the future life: (1) that there is an entity which will continue without a body after death, a discarnate but immortal soul; (2) that after death this entity the soul will be united with another body; (3) that God restores to the person, life continuous with the life the person had before death.

In the first two cases, the continuity of being between the earthly, human existence, and the existence after death is sought in the soul. This means that the human being is essentially soul. It means that soul as the essence of the human is maintained after death, whatever happens to the body. Whether the soul is set free from its body at death and remains thereafter without a body, or whether after death, it will receive another body, the point of the doctrine is to say that the soul is immortal. This was the teaching of Plato, who provided arguments to demonstrate it. That many people, apart from Christian believers, believed that it was possible to prove the doctrine of the immortal soul should give us pause, since that means that it is not distinctively Christian teaching, even when accepted by Christians.

Christian writers for many centuries reckoned seriously that the doctrine of the immortality of the soul was true, and that it could express the Christian hope. If, however the soul is immortal by nature, and if it will after death move inevitably to a different level of being, precisely what is the *Christian* hope? That is to say, what need is there to connect the idea of an *inherently* immortal soul with God as Creator and Redeemer, with the event of his action in Jesus Christ?

We turn then to a third possibility, namely that immortality is a gift of God which either has been or will be bestowed upon man, but which is not man's by nature. As life is *now* the gift of the Creator, so immortality *will be* the gift of be Creator after death. Death is final and human life is significant. As God is good and is the source of all good, so he will bestow life which is good, eternal and immortal if and as he wills. So there is some difficulty with the following position which speaks of immortality as both natural and as conditional.

'For those theists who hold that the soul is naturally immortal also hold that the omnipotent God could if he wished abolish the souls he has made. Their immortality does not give them independence over against their Maker, but only sets them outside the natural mortality of physical organisms.'[21]

The problem is that to say immortality is natural to man means that man is *essentially* immortal. That is to say that he is not subject to final extinction. He is then precisely *not* capable of being abolished. There is no contradiction in claiming that when God created man, he gave him the capacity to become independent, gave him a certain freedom to do what God did not will. But there *is* a contradiction in saying both that God created man immortal and that man is naturally immortal. To say that man is naturally immortal gives man independence over against God. The assertion that God is Creator is incompatible with it. Any immortality which is man's by nature cannot at the same time be the gift of the Creator. To say that God gives man immortality is to define that immortality as dependent upon God. To speak of man as naturally immortal conflicts with the claim that man is creature, and as creature is dependent upon God the Creator. Hence the claim (which 'those theists' make) that such natural immortality does not give the creature independence over against the Creator does not seem to be true.

God grants immortality as he wills. It is his gift. Man is not naturally immortal.

This is the point of the Fall story of *Genesis* chapter three. Man has partaken of the forbidden fruit, and now knows good and evil: 'and now lest he put forth his hand and take also of the tree of life, and eat, and live forever — therefore the LORD God sent him forth from the Garden of Eden' (*Genesis* 3:22, 23). This depicts man

---

21 John Hick, *Death and Eternal Life*. London: William Collins, 1976, p.181.

Death, Immortality, and Resurrection

as created and as fallen as precisely *not* naturally immortal. 'Those theists' to whom John Hick refers in his observation are guilty of the inconsistency and confusion of affirming both that man is by nature immortal and that this immortality is conditioned on the will of God. It is a consistent position to maintain that God created man and so man is dependent. Should man receive immortality it will be because God wills it. He may not do so. But it seems a contradiction to say that God may possibly destroy the immortal life which is natural to man.

If this is so then the teaching sometimes called universalism may be seriously questioned. Universalism is the teaching that in the end, all of God's creatures will come to fulfil his purpose and so participate in the immortality which is his to bestow, and which he does bestow upon condition of response to his love.

Why question this teaching? If God wills to give immortality, he may wish to cause conditions which drive people to respond to his love. If so why has he waited so long? Why could he not have done this at the creation and during the long period of our human history? If God could have created human beings to choose always to do the good rather than the evil, why did he not do so? The answer is that there is a contradiction in the idea of creating free beings who cannot but respond in one way rather than another. If he cannot do so at creation God cannot do so at the end. The ethical problem does not change because death has intervened. The contradiction remains. It is the contradiction between beings being free and not being able to take one of two alternatives. The other then becomes an unreal alternative. If I can only always choose one of two alternatives, the one I do not choose is not a real alternative. If I can only always chose the good, because that is the way I have been created, then the evil is not an alternative. But to do good, I must be able to choose between good and evil. If I am not able to do good or evil, I am not able to do good. Either I am able to do good or evil, or I am not able to do good or evil.

6 Meaning of *soul*

As we now turn to consider the various meanings of the term 'soul,' we shall begin with a statement by John Calvin who wrote 'that man consists of a soul and a body ought to be beyond controversy. Now I understand by the term 'soul' an immortal yet created essence, which is his nobler part. Sometimes it is called 'spirit.' He proceeds to speak of the soul as 'something essential separate from the body.' 'The soul is an incorporeal substance ... set in the body it dwells there as in a house.'[22]

Nothing could be farther from the statement of Gordon Kaufman, quoted earlier, which claimed that it was meaningless to speak of an entity called 'soul' as the dualists did.

We shall now ask what the term 'soul' means, what the phrase 'the immortality of the soul' means, and in particular when the immortality of the soul is religiously significant.

First, note that survival is not equivalent to immortality, since there need be nothing permanent about survival. If the soul is immortal, the soul survives, but if survival is to have religious significance it cannot be mere survival, merely existing again. So definition of the term 'soul' is called for since the term 'soul' serves to identify what it is that survives, what it is that is immortal. It is important to specify what the soul is, for if it is to have religious significance what survives (the soul) must be identifiable.

We can do so by asking simply, 'Would the person live again if the soul survived?' To answer that question we must plot the meanings of the words 'person' and 'soul.' Sometimes we use these words as synonyms, as for example when we speak of a person being a 'good soul' or a 'poor soul.' Here the word 'soul' means 'person.' It is a quite common usage. S.O.S. means, 'Come and rescue *us*'! To cry, 'Save our souls' means, 'We *persons* will perish if we do not get help.'

Sometimes we make a clear distinction between the meaning of 'soul' and 'person.' Calvin gave a quite particular meaning to the

---

22 *Institutes*, I. xv. 2, 6.

term 'soul.' He thought of it as 'an incorporeal substance,' different from the body. Soul, on this understanding is the essential constituent of the person. This dualistic view separates body and soul, and claims that the soul is the 'real person.' This gives us a convenient third term, the term 'real person' which is a designation of 'soul,' standing for an entity which exists in its own right. The classic philosophic expression is in René Descartes (see below, Chapter VII, *Cartesian Dualism*). The dualistic view claims that the soul or the 'real person' can exist independent of the body.

Second, there is the other view which identifies the soul with the person as the psycho-physical unity, the distinctive human consciousness. The human person, traditionally called 'man,' is a soul. 'Soul' is person. The word 'soul' means person. As human beings we are a unity. We are a psycho-somatic unity. It is this unique unity which constitutes us human. 'Soul' is used for the unity which constitutes man personal. The word 'soul' means person and not the essential person conceived as a separable mental entity, the '*real* person' as in the dualist understanding.

Great care is needed in the use of the terms 'person' and 'soul.' This is why we need to use the term 'real person' to make a very important distinction. Granted the distinction between 'person' and 'real person'; the term 'soul' is sometimes used for both now to mean the one ('person') and sometimes to mean the other ('real person'). Hence there is a recurring ambiguity.

The two sentences, 'The person survives.' 'The soul survives.' *may* mean the same thing or they may not. It depends upon whether the word 'soul' means 'person' or whether it means 'real person,' the incorporeal essence (as in Calvin and Descartes). Their meaning is identical, when 'soul' means 'person,' or opposed, when 'soul' means 'real person.'

The accompanying chart enumerates the three possible meanings which the claim, 'The soul is immortal' may have.

Explanation of terms used in the chart.

The term 'soul' can have two meanings: First, it may mean the person, the psycho-somatic unity which constitutes the human being. It can also mean 'real person' (RP), an entity existing in its own right,' i.e. separable from body. S stands for soul in the former sense. S_s means soul as an entity separable from body. B means Body. So B_h means human body. P means person, a psycho-physical unity.

	Life	**After Life**
Model A	$P = B_h + S_s$	$S_s - B_h, \rightarrow S_s + B^2$
Model B	$P = B_h + S_s\ (=RP)$	$S_s \rightarrow S_s\ (=RP) - B_h$
Model C	$P = S, S = P$	$P = S, S = P$

Model A. The psycho-physical unity is constituted by human body and soul. The soul is a separable entity. At death, the dissolution of human body occurs. The separation of soul (S the soul as separate entity) from human body (B_h) takes place. Soul is re-incarnated into another body (B_2).

The person is a union of body and soul. Soul is separable from body in the sense that it may be transferred from the human body to another body. At death the soul is separated from its earthly body to be put within another body. There is no separate incorporeal existing of the soul. After death another being comes into existence. Theories of re-incarnation suggest the possibility of many different kinds of material body into which the soul may be placed. Most are less than 'personal.' The common thread is that soul requires a body, a material substance, for its continued existence.

Model B. Dualism. The soul is the real entity (RP), united in this existence with a human body. At death the body ceases to exist, call this the 'removal of the body, -B_h. The disembodied soul survives, i.e. the immaterial soul as the real entity, the real person.

When soul means 'real person' or essence' that essence can exist after death. This is the dualistic view. The body and the soul are different and separable entities, and the soul can and will exist apart from the body. The body is a fetter and at death the soul is released from that fetter. So the real person, hemmed in by the body in this existence, is released for its existence after life. Model B is that of the immortality or survival of the soul in a disembodied existence.

Model C. 'Person' and 'soul' are synonyms, meaning 'the person,' i.e. the psycho-somatic unity which constitutes the human being. At death there takes place an act from beyond the human which resurrects or replicates the person, the soul. On this interpretation *person* and *soul* have the same meaning. These terms are here used for the psycho-somatic unity which is the person. What is human is the person. What survives is the person. There is no talk of the separation of distinct entities. The human person is a unity. Model C serves for the resurrection of the person. It represents the meaning of the term *soul* in the Biblical usage. *Nephesh* and *psuche* are characteristically used in this sense of the person or the self.

Our human existence is varied. We sing and dance, cry and fight, create works of art, play games, quarrel, etc. What relation does the future existence have to the present, often rich and full, always concrete, human existence? If we are to talk of individual human immortality, there must be some continuity between this human person and the reality which survives. The chart indicated the possibility of disembodied existence after death (Model B). But that would not be *human* existence. How could a disembodied soul be identified with a particular human person? Unless we can make this identification, the existence of disembodied souls is not relevant to the question of the immortality of the individual human being.

What conditions have to be fulfilled, therefore, so that we may know that the person after death is the same as the person who lived, remembering that the person who lived was an individual with quite specific experiences and memories? Can disembodied existence be conceived in such a way that it is intelligible as personal human existence in continuity with a previous human existence? Can embodied existence be so conceived?

The tokens which we recognise as constituting proof of a person's identity are on the one hand bodily features, some marks carried from birth, some scar or other, height, shape, features of the eye, fingerprints. On the other hand are the person's memories. We would say of another that he was the same person if we were convinced that he had the same memories as the person we know, let us say, about things that only he and we had in common. When I ask the first person question, (i.e. How do I know that I am the same person that I was?), I then look into my past and co-ordinate my memories (I may have kept a diary) with my past experiences, and with the reports of other people. No particle in our body is the same as it was a few years ago. Our identity does not depend upon such identity of physical matter. So the presence of the same memory would be a proper identifying feature and would enable us to establish that we were the same person as we had been.

When we assert life after death in continuity with this life we think that conceiving survival as human, individual consciousness is not an insuperable obstacle. We believe that we can make intelligible the idea of survival (embodied or disembodied) as the survival of an individual human being. Or, we may ask whether it in the end matters whether we can or not.

7 God raises the dead

Finally, we should note that for the idea of immortality to have religious significance, it must be related to belief in God.

We must make an important distinction in talking of immortality. It is one not emphasised in the context from which the passage of John Hick was quoted. For, when the Christian sets immortality within a theistic context he speaks of resurrection. The understanding that God is the source of all life and that immortality is God's gift to man receives distinctive expression in the statement that God would raise the dead. All the living die. But beyond the fact of death is the resurrection of the dead. That will be God's act, as the resurrection of Jesus from the dead was God's act.

Death, Immortality, and Resurrection 69

It will be when the dead are resurrected that the gift of immortality will be given.

Traditional Christian teaching has here introduced an ethical consideration. For our present human life is a testing ground and we make of that life something worthy or unworthy. God is gracious and immortality will be his gift, as life here and now is his gift. It will be his future gift in view of what man makes of his gift here and now. So the notion of a judgment came to be connected with the idea of resurrection, and the whole range of related questions formed the context of a particular concern of theology, the doctrine of the last things, or eschatology as it came to be called (from the Greek work *eschaton* meaning 'last').

God raises the dead. God raises the dead to immortal life. So the Christian may speak of resurrection to personal immortality, with all that that involves in terms of relationships beyond the individual. The resurrection and the immortality are God's gift, God's act. On this understanding, in contrast to that of the immortality of the soul, we speak of soul as the real person. An intelligible and consistent doctrine of creation (God is source of all and man is dependent) and of grace (God gives life) is then possible. Immortality is not inevitable. We confuse the issue if we speak of the 'natural immortality of the soul,' since we are ignoring the fact, as bluntly stated clearly above by Gordon Kaufman, and argued for and expounded in our text, and in direct contrast to Calvin, that it is beyond doubt that man does *not* consist of a soul and a body.

8 God is immortal

Christian theists use the term *immortal* not only of man, to express the hope of surviving death. They also say of God that he is immortal. To say that God is immortal assumes that we speak meaningfully of God by taking elements drawn from our experience and using them. Since the Christian theist believes that God is other than man, he cannot simply predicate human qualities of him in a straightforward way. So he duly qualifies what he says when he uses such terms to speak of God.

Some of the attributes of human beings and the characteristics of human experience are applied to God, but the Christian theist tries to make sure that they are not misunderstood. So he qualifies the terms he uses. He says, for example, that God is Father. He then qualifies the term 'father' to exclude those meanings he does not consider appropriate. For not all fathers are wise and good. He says God is a good father, a heavenly father, a living father. With each of these qualifications a contrast is drawn to what human fathers sometimes are like. He speaks of the wisdom of God and then goes on to say that God is '*most* wise' or '*all* wise.'

There are other ways in which he can make his qualifications. Man is mortal. God is immortal. He can deny of God what he affirms of human beings. The expression which results, in this case 'immortal,' serves as a pointer, as a symbol. We have taken a human characteristic and denied it of God. This suggests that God is other then man in respect of man's mortality. But *how* is God other? What is the gulf that separates him from us, and us from him?

Suppose I say, 'You can distinguish James from John in the following way. James is healthy but John is unhealthy.' What I have done is to put the negative '-un' in front of 'healthy.' I indicate by so doing that that something which applies to James does not apply to John. Of course both James and John are human. In this case we are drawing contrasts within the realm of the human.

But there is another distinction in the case of God, and that is why we say that the negative term which results is a pointer. God is not other than man merely in the fact that man dies and God does not. That man dies and God does not is a manifestation of a different order of being on man's part and on God's. That God is immortal is an aspect of his different order of being.

So, when we say that God is immortal, we mean that because God is other than man it is necessary to deny of God what we assert of the human. We assert that man is mortal. By saying that God is immortal we are pointing to the fact that God is of a different order

Death, Immortality, and Resurrection

of being from man. When we negate of God what we say of man, we point to this different order, this otherness. The theologians call this otherness, God's transcendence. The putting of the negative prefix before 'mortal' as well as putting the negative in front of a whole lot of other adjectives, points to the fact that God's being is of a different order from our being. So God is said to be *in*-visible, *im*-passive, *un*-changeable etc.[23] Because *so many* human characteristics are qualified in this way, we stress the idea that God is other than we are, and that such terms are symbols of that transcendent reality rather than descriptions of it.

'God is immortal' means that death, dying, dissolution do not apply to God because God is not the sort of reality to which they could apply. That contrasts with human reality. Human being is that sort of being to which the term 'mortal' always applies. When the term 'immortal' is used of the human reality that does not mean that man is not mortal. He is. But the term 'mortal' is not at all appropriate of God. To say God is immortal is to deny that the term 'mortal' can be applied to him in any sense. It is to deny that he is in any way mortal. That is what the New Testament writer meant when he said that God 'alone has immortality' (*I Timothy* 6:16). God is set apart from the creatures. He is other than they. So the Christian theist uses the words 'holy' and 'eternal' of him. These expressions lay stress upon his otherness. They express the claim that his order of being is transcendent to the human. That God is holy, other than we are, is the basis of our hope that we may be other than we are, that — to use another New Testament expression — we may be 'like him' (*I John* 3:2), that is to say, that we may participate in the being which he provides for us.

This leads us to an important distinction and to what is an important paradox. Traditional Christian teaching has very emphatically insisted upon the distinction between God's being and man's being. One way of putting the distinction is by saying that God is necessary and that man is contingent. The being of God

---

23 We would have to look more carefully at such expressions were our purpose here a different one.

does not depend on somewhat other than himself. In contrast to this the being of man is dependent. Man is what he is by virtue of his having been created. God is what he is by virtue of himself. In him is life unborrowed, underived. Our life is derived from his life. We are what we are by virtue of his gift. God is Creator and man is creature. To this there corresponds the distinction between God's immortality and man's immortality. Should man be immortal, it will be due to God and not because man is immortal in himself, by nature. God is gracious and we as humans depend upon that grace. Should we aspire to immortality, it will be because God grants us that immortality, and not because we have an innate immortality, a certain independence of God. God grants to us what is in himself underived. It is clear that the term 'immortal' is used rather differently of God than it is used of man. This difference can be put by saying that God is not immortal in the same sense that man is immortal. God is immortal and does not cease to be. Man may be immortal, but does die. God is immortal because he is himself the source of life. Man is immortal only if and when he receives the gift of renewed life from God. It is of God's good grace that man receives the gift of immortality. Man has no life in himself. He is mortal.

We have now arrived at the same conclusion that we had reached in the earlier part of the chapter, but from a different viewpoint.

9 Four alternatives

Various alternatives are open to us as we consider further the problems raised by the preceding discussion. Having gone thus far we may feel that it is time to stop. We may feel that we cannot go on profitably because whatever we may say from now on will be uncertain speculation about things we cannot know. Since we lack certainty, we may feel that it would not be worthwhile to continue. To go on would be academic, in the sense that we have no sure way of deciding between the possible alternatives. But it is only as

Death, Immortality, and Resurrection

we set the alternatives in front of ourselves that we can make our decision concerning them.

That man is mortal is consistent with the following assertions: (1) All die: none live again. Death is final. (2) All die: all live again, this time an immortal life. (3) All die: some live again, this time an immortal life. (4) All die: some live again only to perish; others live again, this time an immortal life. (5) Only some live again. (6) None live again.

We must make a further distinction in view of the Christian teachings about heaven, hell and judgment. Life that is immortal is not by definition and necessarily a life of bliss. It might be a life of pain. Teaching about punishment coupled with that of innate immortality would condemn the wicked to an immortality of suffering.

We have now introduced the idea of punishment and of judgment. One's fate after death, in Christianity, as in many other religious traditions, is said to hinge on the way in which one has lived one's days and used one's opportunities in this life. Not to use this life well is to sin, and it is due to the human agent what will be his condition at the end. He will be duly rewarded, that is to say, punished, for his sin. But since life cannot be assessed until it is complete, the decision concerning the tenor, the status, of that life and person can be made only after it is finished. So from Augustine (AD 354-430) onwards, Christian teachers began to elaborate a scheme of last day events connected with the judgment.

But where is one to place the judgment in relation to rewards and punishments? Will the judgment take place at the last day, or will it take place at death? Does one become immortal at death and go then to reward or to punishment? If that is the case, what of the judgment? Has that already taken place or is it a superfluous appendage after all have gone to their reward? What sense *then* does it make to speak of the *Last* Judgment?

The alternative is to put the judgment later, and to reserve God's decision about and his effecting of rewards and punishments to that later point. This involves saying that death, the end of human consciousness, marks the beginning of a transitional period at the end of which there will be renewal of life. The renewed life will then be either of bliss or pain. The alternative is extinction. Heaven and Hell are names given to these alternatives. If there is judgment at the end then there seems no point why the dead go to their reward or punishment at death. Life would be renewed to them at the end so that the great showdown can take place. If that is the case and at the resurrection the dead receive reward or punishment, they will either have been judged in the intermediate time, or they will be judged after they have been raised. In the former case, they do not 'stand before the judgment seat of God.' They receive their reward when they are resurrected at the end. The just Judge has pronounced sentence and the Last Judgment puts it into effect.

We have considered two alternative possibilities namely, first, that one goes to one's reward at death; second, that one goes to one's reward after an interim period bounded at the one end by death and at the other by resurrection But these do not exhaust the possible alternatives. Others are based on the understanding of the interim period as a transitional one. Let us see how this intermediate state has sometimes been conceived.

Sometimes it is understood as a time of renewed opportunities. One will have the chance to make the necessary improvements before becoming fit for the bliss of heaven. This intermediate state is sometimes called purgatory. This intermediate state refines man and readies him for heavenly bliss. Those who believe that all enter this state and eventually become fit for heaven may not speak of it as purgatory. They are known as universalists. All, they say, ultimately attain to a readiness for the gift of eternal life.

A fourth alternative is to say that death is a transition but that we do not have any clear analogies to describe the state of consciousness (or lack of it) which then emerges. It looks as though the Old Testament understanding of *sheol* was some such condition — a dull, misty region of muted consciousness, a kind of sub-human existence.

Death, Immortality, and Resurrection

This understanding of the state of man in death is to be found in many passages in the Old Testament. For the Hebrew, the word soul, *nephesh* (as we have seen) means man as he is alive and active. The soul, *nephesh*, is not considered distinct from the body. Nowhere in the Old Testament do we find that the soul is immortal, or that man after death is incorruptible. The dead go to *sheol*, 'a land which is not a land,' 'the realm which is not.' It is a realm 'where God is not.' 'None talk of thee among the dead; who praises thee in sheol?' *Psalm* 6:5. The dead remained in Sheol, the not-land, only for a certain time. 'When that time was over, then it was as if the person had never been. The life of the Hebrew was at an end. Only God knows of him always.'[24] In the wisdom books of the Old Testament, such a belief in this continued shadow-existence is abandoned. Death is the absolute end of man. 'Men have no advantage over beasts ... All go to the same place: all come from the dust, and to the dust all return,' 'If a man dies, shall he live again? He shall never be raised from his sleep.' (*Ecclesiastes* 3:19, *Job* 14:12). Since this understanding was surpassed both in later Hebrew thinking and in the Christian hope, we shall not consider it further.

10 Four guiding considerations

This brief survey suffices to show that to differentiate and to assess the Christian teachings of the various kinds, some principle of evaluation is needed. How is the after-death existence to be ordered? Who will and who will not receive life after death? On what grounds does one decide whether the light of life will be extinguished, whether we enjoy eternal bliss or suffer eternal pain? On what basis does one decide whether ultimately all human beings will attain to eternal life or will not? Indeed, how does one decide whether there is an interim state between death and eternal life and if there is what that interim state will be like?

---

24 Ludwig Kohler, *Hebrew Man*. London: S.C.M Press, 1956. p. 113.

We propose four such considerations to guide us in coming to our conclusions. First, moral considerations. Even if it is not always evident, there is a moral order of things, in which the goodness of God is manifest and is clearly seen. No satisfying account of death can he given which ignores such moral considerations.

Second, talk of resurrection and of judgment must be clearly coordinated with talk of immortality and of death. When this is not done we must remain dissatisfied.

Third, we must make intelligible the possibility of an after-death state. This means that we must be able so speak with some degree of clarity about it. But what concepts shall we use? How shall we guide our imagination? What, if any, evidence is there to which we can appeal to enable us to fill in the details? For example, is the next existence conceivable in the body as some form of physical existence? Or, shall we attempt to conceive it as spiritual? Since human life is inconceivable without the relationships which the body makes possible, how shall we speak meaningfully of post-mortem existence without such relationships?

When we have given our answers to such questions we shall then be in a position to compare them. For example, if we can satisfactorily imagine a bodiless state which provides for a personal and satisfying human life, then we must give due consideration to such.[25] We might however prefer to say that we are quite justified in believing that we can neither conceive nor imagine what the after-death state of immortality will be like. But that position itself needs justification and will not be convincing unless one can provide good reason for accepting it.[26]

Fourth, what we say will harmonise with the insights of normative Christian interpretation of life after death. That involves

---

25 Such an account is provided by H.H. Price in his article, 'The Problem of Life After Death' in Terence Penelhum (editor). *Immortality*. Belmont, California: Wadsworth Publishing Company Inc., 1973, pp. 103-117.

26 Cf. Maurice Wiles, *The Remaking of Christian Doctrine*. London: S.C.M. Press, 1974, pp. 143,144, where he argues that the 'conceivability criterion cannot be rigorously applied in this area.' What does it mean not to apply it rigorously?

making a judgment as to what is normative Christian interpretation, and so brings us to a consideration of the relevant passages of the New Testament, in particular in relation to the 'resurrection body' and to the ways in which such teachings have been developed and interpreted in Christian thought.

IV Resurrection and Immortality

1 Are they compatible?

Christians have often used the language both of resurrection and of immortality to express the hope they have for life after death. It is true that some have set resurrection in opposition to immortality and, either by explicit argument by emphasis or by implication or silence, have clearly preferred the one to the other. For, there are ways of understanding these respective ideas so that the one excludes the other, or makes the use of the one inconsistent with the other.[27]

For example, it is inconsistent to speak of the soul as (1) innately immortal, that is to say immortal unconditionally by nature, and (2) as distinct from the body and able to exist without the body, indeed only able to exist without the body, and (3) to say that death is the point at which the soul escapes from the mortal impediment which imprisoned it during this life, there being no more place for a body of any sort, and (4) to speak of a resurrection of the body. This is true whether the ideas are expressed in Christian terms or not.

Resurrection is incompatible with immortality since the former is of the body which is restored to life, and the latter is of the soul which does not and cannot perish because it is in essence non-bodily and imperishable. The definition and the use of the terms in this way have led to a fundamental contradiction. There are, of course, other particular ways in which Christian teaching may prove to be inconsistent. If the soul is unconditionally immortal it *must* continue to exist after death of the body. So it goes to its reward at death. Then, to speak of resurrection *at the last day*,

---

27 Maurice Wiles insists that this should not be done. He notes that it has been the case that traditional Christian teaching has given the idea of resurrection the priority. He himself gives reasons for questioning this position. See *Ibid.*, pp. 125-146.

before the ultimate state is introduced, appears unnecessary and contradictory. If resurrection at the last day is to be meaningful, it will serve to introduce a new state of affairs.

Attempts are made to bridge this gap by speaking of an intermediate state between death and the last day, such that the real change will be made only at the end. But there is a basic confusion in attempting *in this way* to co-ordinate the ideas of resurrection and immortality.

We question the need to set the idea of resurrection against the idea of immortality. The New Testament uses both kinds of language, and with good reason. So we can state a position which is not contradictory and which at the same time preserves a distinctive place and function for both kinds of language, immortality language pointing to something to which resurrection language does not, and vice versa. Both together will serve to express the Christian understanding of God, namely that all life, here and hereafter, has its source in him.

2 God takes the initiative

Whether we speak, then, of immortality or of resurrection, the initiative in the matter in any case is with God. God is the source of the immortality which he bestows upon man according to his will.

This priority of God is expressed in the Christian teaching of creation. God brought man into being and provided for him the possibility of a continuing life. God is the source and end of all that man has and is, will have and will be. If man shall be immortal, that immortality will still be the gift of God. The Christian does not speak of an immortality independent of God and of his grace. God is transcendent and grants to man what, apart from the gift, he would not receive. If man shall be immortal, it will be because God grants him that gift.

Similarly, the Christian insists, that it is God who raises the dead. Without the act of God in raising the dead, those who have died would no longer live. Death is final. The dissolution of the

Death, Immortality, and Resurrection 81

body becomes complete. It is in view of this finality that resurrection has great significance. Unless God takes the initiative there will be no renewal of life. By speaking of the resurrection of the dead, the Christian makes the claim that God *will* take the initiative. The dead will live again, not by some inherent power which resides in the nature of man, but because God creatively restores human life.

3 Two kinds of language

What of the life which man will receive from God? Is it to be an endless life? Or will man perish again (like the people who were raised died again in the biblical stories)? If man perishes again will there be another resurrection, or this time oblivion?

God raises the dead to an immortal life, according to his grace. Clearly, merely to be brought back to life again does not constitute Christian hope. It is necessary to add that the resurrection is to life *immortal*, and then to qualify the term 'immortal' so that no confusion or contradiction results.

We have distinguished several ways now in which the idea of immortality can he deployed. We should differentiate in particular between innate immortality, immortality of the soul and conditional immortality.

Innate immortality means that it is the essential nature of man that he is immortal. Immortality is a defining feature of human beings. It is not bestowed as a gift, nor is it an accident. It is an essential and independent feature of his humanity. Man simply is immortal.

Immortality of the soul, as understood traditionally in Christian teaching, assumes a duality of body and soul. Human being is defined in relation to this dualism. The soul is the real person, the permanent and essential reality. So the point at which the soul is freed from the body is itself the beginning of reality. For this all else is preparation. The term 'soul,' thus used in distinction from 'body' or 'person,' means an intellectual entity (mind, *nous*) or a spiritual entity (spirit, *pneuma*). In any case, it is other than the body and not, as we now say, the whole man, the psycho-somatic unity, the person that we know.

But, confusion is possible. The phrase 'the immortality of the soul' may mean the immortality of the person, since the word 'soul' may mean 'person,' as when we speak of a 'poor soul.'

The term *conditional immortality* means that it is not an essential feature of human nature that we are immortal. It means that survival of death is neither automatic, nor necessarily universal. It puts a question mark against the assertion of universal salvation, what is often called universalism. As human persons we have the capacity for immortality, but if the capacity is to be realised, certain conditions will be fulfilled. The primary condition is that God is gracious and that God raises the dead. We are 'candidates for immortality.' Our immortality is potential and not endemic, bestowed and received, not essential. For the Christian, man is a child of God, dependent upon God for life now and hereafter.

We can co-ordinate the ideas of resurrection and immortality, since we have made the necessary distinctions. God raises the human person to life, which life, according to his will, is an immortal life. Death is final. Man is dependent on God. So we can employ both concepts, immortality and resurrection, in a meaningful way.

But we have by no means exhausted the problems involved in using *both* terms. We can now ask in what ways the language of both immortality and resurrection may express the particular and distinctive Christian hope. How is such hope related to the resurrection of Jesus Christ and to the claim that God raised Jesus Christ from the dead? Can we by considering the change that took place at the resurrection of Jesus Christ come to understand that change that takes place at the resurrection of the believer?

For the Christian, immortal life is dependent but eternal and not subject to death. God raises the dead to immortal life. That the life to which the person is raised is immortal is what distinguishes it from the life which has been lived. Thus immortality is reserved for the resurrection life. So Paul emphasises the change that will occur at the resurrection. He contemplated the possibility that those who

Death, Immortality, and Resurrection

live at the last day will participate in a transformation. That transformation introduces immortality. For both those who live until the last day and those who have previously died, immortality is then bestowed. 'We shall not all sleep, but we shall all be changed, in a moment, in the twinkling of an eye, at the last trumpet. For the trumpet shall sound, and the dead will be raised imperishable, and we shall be changed. For this perishable nature must put on the imperishable, and this mortal nature must put on immortality.' (*I Corinthians* 15:51-53). The change is from the mortal to the immortal. Such a change is necessary because man is not now immortal. Nor does 'the perishable inherit the imperishable' (v. 50).

The Christian claims that all hope for life after death is due to Jesus Christ. This is put, as we might expect, in the language of immortality. God has manifested his purpose and grace 'through the appearing of our Saviour Jesus Christ, who abolished death and brought life and immortality to light through the Gospel' (*I Timothy* 1:10). It is also put, as we have just seen, in the language of resurrection.

4 A QUALITATIVE DIFFERENCE

Now an interesting fact emerges. The language of resurrection is not only used of the transition from death to life. It is used, metaphorically, of the transition from a life before Christian faith to a life of Christian faith. It is also when so used connected with the resurrection of Jesus Christ. 'For we know that Christ being raised from the dead will never die again; death no longer has dominion over him. The death he died he died to sin, once for all, but the life he lives he lives to God. So you also must consider yourselves dead to sin and alive to God in Christ Jesus.' (*Romans* 6:7-11).

The transition from a life without faith to Christian faith is like dying and being raised from the dead. The new life is of a quite different quality than the old life. The contrast could not be greater. Many different figures of speech are used to portray how great the change is. Slavery is replaced by freedom. Serving one master in replaced by serving another. From being an alien one becomes a citizen. One moves from darkness to light. A former way of life has become otiose and moribund. Such is the magnitude of the change that has taken place that we cannot compare the new with the old. It is qualitatively different.

So we have two sets of contrasts. On the one hand, the contrast between the life outside faith and the life of faith, and on the other the contrast between the present mortal life and the immortal life that shall be after death. The same language which signifies passing from the present mortal life to immortal life is used to signify the passing from the life without faith to the life of faith — the language of resurrection.

The symbol of baptism is linked with the idea of resurrection used as a symbol of the coming of Christian faith. 'We were buried therefore with him by baptism into death, that as Christ was raised from the dead by the glory of the Father, we too might walk in newness of life' (*Romans* 6:4).

There is a qualitative difference between this life and the life to come. There is a qualitative difference between life outside of Jesus Christ and life in him. The new life, even here and now is *eternal* life. It is a characteristic teaching of the New Testament that such eternal life, life in relationship with God, has its beginning now.

5 Eternal life?

The Jews understood 'eternal life' as future, as life in the age to come. In fact, Jesus used the term in this sense, for example in *Mark* 10:30, when he says that his disciples would receive 'in the age to come eternal life.' Jesus also used the term 'Kingdom of God' frequently. Sometimes he referred to it as the future and sometimes as the present life. In the Gospel of John, the phrase 'eternal life' has such a double reference, that is to say it refers both to the future and to the present. So a commentator can write of its meaning in this Gospel: 'The concept (eternal life) retains something of its original

Death, Immortality, and Resurrection

eschatological connection ... but it may equally be thought of as a present gift of God; in this *zoe aionios* in *John* resembles 'kingdom of God' in the synoptic Gospels. That which is properly a future blessing becomes a present fact in virtue of the realisation of the future in Christ'[28] (see II, 11 above).

'To know' both in the Old and New Testaments means 'to be in relationship with.' To be in relationship with God in Jesus Christ is to enjoy a quality of life which is both incomparable and unsurpassable. Some Old Testament writers had glimpsed the insight that one could 'know' God. They knew a relationship with Yahweh and this assured them that there was hope that this relationship would be maintained even though death intervened. They dared to hope with assurance that this was so. The grounds for such a faith are in God alone. If man is able to know a personal, individual relationship with God, who is the Source of life, then there is hope for overcoming the power of death. Belief in immortality is only possible where personal religion is in evidence, where there is a relation between God and man which man recognises as the power and the love of God.

It was the insight and experience of the great prophets of the Old Testament that man can know the will of God. One may go so far as to say that 'the primary substance of Old Testament revelation ... is not knowledge *about* God but knowledge *of* God.'[29] It is this which enables the prophet to see beyond death to a renewal of the relationship he had with Yahweh.

This is given a decided Christian flavour in the New Testament, where faith in Jesus Christ provides a quality of life, 'life in the spirit' (to use the Pauline phrase), 'eternal life' (to use the Johannine), such that that quality, that relationship, provides the

---

28 C.K.Barrett, *The Gospel according to St. John*. London: S.P.C.K., 1956. p. 179.
29 R.B.Y.Scott, *The Relevance of the Prophets*. New York: The Macmillan Company, 1944. p. 212. W. O. E. Oesterley and T. Robinson, *Hebrew Religion. Its Origin and Development*. London: S.P.C.K., 1955. p. 357.

decisive and important clue to the nature of life after death, and assures the believer of its reality. It will be a life 'with God.'

PART II

Introduction

Among the several claims that we have made in Part One are the following:

A human being is a unity.

We should avoid dualistic talk which divides human being into two separate parts, body and soul.

At death the human person ceases to exist and the body is dissolved.

There is no immaterial thing which survives as the real self.

If human persons survive, it will be because God resurrects them.

Our task now is to make sense of these assertions. That means that we must provide and examine arguments to explain them. We have therefore certain outstanding tasks to perform, such as the following:

To explain what it means to be a psycho-somatic unity.

To examine what personal identity means and if possible to indicate what constitutes personal identity.

To find an acceptable way of conceiving the idea of resurrection for persons.

To ask whether the person surviving death is the same person as lived an earthly existence.

To ask whether personal identity is necessary for a religious doctrine of survival.

To ask whether the qualitative change at resurrection (as Paul conceives it in *I Corinthians* 15) is compatible with the emergence of the same person to new life after death.

Examining the 'replica' theory and asking, 'Would the replica be me?' and 'Would such a reconstruction of the self satisfy resurrection hope?'

So we are led into questions about bodily and psychological continuity, questions about the sameness of the self and other thorny problems connected with survival. Would we want to survive if we were not the 'same' selves as we were here? But how is it possible, assuming we have some idea of what it is to be the same self after death, that we shall be the same self after death, when it is impossible that we shall have the same physical body we had? The alternative seems to be that if we have anything like personal identity, it will be some sort of replication of the unity of memories, desires and feelings we once had, which we are now having. But such qualitative identity is not the same as numerical identity. So what does continued existence of the person, i.e. being the same self, (even after a break in consciousness) consist in? Unless we can give a reasonable answer to this question, we shall be unable to conceive of a reasonable doctrine of resurrection.

It is to these problems that we address ourselves in Part Two.

Part two is philosophical. Our procedure here is to develop a series of arguments leading to conclusions concerning soul, person and survival. This involves us in using an established terms, and using them with care. It is within the philosophical discussions of Western philosophy that such language has developed. So we intend to discuss some of the major philosophical treatments of the subjects which interest us as a means of clarifying the issues and explaining the language and as a means of providing a background for our own argument which will follow the survey of the leading philosophers.

So, first we set out problems and possible approaches to them.

Second, we survey the philosophical positions critically.

Third, we suggest constructive positions and indicate that we can show these to be reasonable. This we shall do in a brief concluding statement.

We have chosen the philosophers we discuss for their intrinsic interest and their relevance to our own exposition: *Plato* (427-347 BC), who defended the doctrine of the soul's immortality; Aristotle (384-322 BC) who conceived the soul in 'functional' terms; *René Descartes* (AD 1596-1650), the father of modern philosophy and proponent of the dualistic understanding of man; his critic, *Gil-*

bert *Ryle* (1900-1976), whose book, *The Concept of Mind* (1949), is the classical criticism of dualism; and lastly *John Hick*'s (1919-) 'replica' theory of the resurrection, based upon an understanding of man as a unity.

V Plato

1 Dualism

Plato was the first philosopher in the West to attempt to provide a series of proofs for the immortality of the soul.[30] To do so he distinguished between body and soul (or mind). The soul is non-bodily, incorporeal and so both different from and capable of independence of the body. The soul is not a harmony of parts, of elements, for 'if the soul is a harmony ..., it must of necessity perish.' If the soul were made up of elements in harmony, when the elements perish, the soul would perish and so there could be no talk of survival. The soul is 'a far more divine thing than a harmony.' It is 'something fitted to lead and rule ... the conditions of the body.' Plato thus distinguishes the bodily parts which perish at death from the soul which survives such dissolution. The soul is non-bodily and non-visible. It is the ruler of the body. It is the self, the 'real person,' the essential person.

Plato was concerned with the question, 'What can we know?' He opposed the sceptics who claimed that we cannot know, that knowledge was beyond our grasp. He was also concerned with the question, 'What is?' or 'What really is?' For him the two questions were indissolubly related. He insisted that if it is real you can know it, and if it's not real you cannot know it. We can know only what is real. So we may be under the illusion that we know when we do not. The scale of knowing and the scale of being correspond. Since sensible things, i.e. things which we apprehend by means of our senses, seeing, hearing etc., for example sights, foods, and sounds, are not really real but as it were mere shadows of what is real we cannot know them. So we could live in a world of shadows. But

---

30 For some of Plato's key passages see Antony Flew, *Body, Mind and Death*. New York: Macmillan, 1973. pp. 4,5,34-71.

this is the world of unreality. We may live in the world of shadows and not know that it is not real. Indeed we may think that it is real.

2 THE SOUL'S KNOWLEDGE AND PRE-EXISTENCE

Plato considered the soul the real person which was imprisoned in the body. Bodily things, pleasures, sensations were opposed to the things of the intellect. The soul was the higher part of this creature who was body and soul. The soul pre-existed and in its pre-existence had knowledge. Plato has Socrates give an empirical demonstration of this in the dialogue *Meno* (see below). The knowledge which the soul had in its pre-existence, Plato was later to say, was knowledge of the Forms. These Forms were the realities behind (so to speak) the individual and particular things. These forms could be known only as the soul separated itself from the bodily and distanced itself from the physical and the pleasures the physical provided, the things of sound, sight and taste. The soul was hooked to the body in this mortal existence. So it was a most difficult thing for the soul to distance itself from the body. It was only possible if one repudiated the sensible pleasures and attempted to live a life of contemplation.

Plato recognised that he did not prove the existence of the pre-existing and immortal soul. In the dialogue *Parmenides*, he presents arguments which show that he was aware of serious objections to his position and that he took account of them. In fact he clearly states what he takes to be his method and the status of his arguments and his argumentative procedure. We make assumptions (his word in Greek is *hypotheseis*). We then show that what follows from such assumptions is reasonable because we have used a rational process to draw conclusions from the assumptions. So what follows is shown thereby to be reasonable. In the process the assumptions are also shown to be reasonable.

The arguments in *Parmenides* are directed toward supporting Plato's theory of Forms on which his claims about the soul depend. A major problem for the Forms concerns how we have knowledge of them, and how that knowledge is related to our sensory experience.

Plato is a *dualist*. He separates reality or 'being' into two kinds. The Greek word for 'Being' is *on* from which we get our English word 'ontological.' Plato contrasts these two kinds. They possess opposing characteristics. This is ontological dualism. By dividing reality into two in this radical way, and tying knowledge so closely with such ontological dualism, he exposes himself to the criticism that we cannot move from one realm of knowledge to the other. We have no knowledge of absolute being in us for absolute essences do not exist in us. Things in the world do not have reference to the Forms but only to one another quite apart from the Forms. The Forms thus become unknowable to us. Plato cannot give an account of the relationship between the Forms and the objects of sensory experience.[31]

The soul is related to unchanging realities. These we think of when we contemplate the Ideas that are eternal, when we contemplate the universals rather than the particulars and the perishing. He argues that since the soul is related to the realm of permanent universals, the soul is itself immortal, and will survive death. When the body decays, the soul will live on forever. The soul is therefore the 'real self,' the 'real person.'

Plato argues that a craftsman uses tools but is different from the tools he uses. So man, that is to say the human person, is different from the hands and eyes he employs in the course of his work. Man is different from the body, which he uses. Man cannot be body, since he uses and rules the body. Man cannot be soul and body, since the body is ruled and the soul rules. So either man is nothing at all, or if something, he turns out to be nothing else than soul. The incorporeal soul is the real self, the real person.

---

31 Plato, *Parmenides*, 133b-135e.

3 Ambiguity of the 'soul'

But Plato did not always distinguish two senses of 'soul.' Sometimes he uses the term 'soul' to mean the principle of life. A soul, in this sense, is something that lives, a living being. But he also uses the word 'soul' (as we have seen) in the sense of the person or the self. It is important to notice that these two meanings of the word 'soul' are quite different from one another. In the one case, it means the principle of life. In the other case, it means the person, the real self. Now let us allow (for the sake of argument) that Plato has established that 'soul' in the sense of the idea of the principle of life is immortal. That does not mean that he has established that 'soul' in the sense of 'real person' is immortal. To demonstrate that the principle of life is eternal is not to establish that the person is immortal. Plato's confusion of the two senses means that this argument does not do what he believes it to have done, namely to have established the immortality of the soul in the sense of the immortality of the disembodied 'real person.'

Plato also argued that things such as horses, ears and knives have particular functions. The function is the particular job that thing can do better than anything else. He then asks what the function of the soul is. He answers that the soul's function is life, to 'govern and manage things well.'

4 Arguments for immortality

In the dialogue, *Phaedo*, Plato presents a series of arguments for the immortality of the soul. One of these is sometimes called the *Argument from Affinity*.[32] Assuming that there are Absolutes, that there is Beauty and Goodness and not just beautiful and good things and actions, what is beautiful is so because it partakes of Beauty. 'Beautiful things are made beautiful by Beauty.' A beautiful object is beautiful because it reflects and exemplifies the Absolute Beauty. A good thing or a good act is good because it reflects and exemplifies Absolute Goodness. Things are beautiful because they

---

32 Plato, *Phaedo*, 100B - 105E. Cf. Flew, *op. cit.*, pp. 55-63.

Death, Immortality, and Resurrection

participate in Beauty. Things are good because they participate in Goodness. Put abstractly, a thing exists by participating in the proper essence of each thing in which it participates. Something is great by reason of greatness and small by reason of smallness, by participating in one or the other. A thing cannot become its own opposite as in the case of snow and fire. Snow is cold, and fire is hot. Cold cannot be hot. The number five will not admit the idea of even, nor the number ten the idea of odd. As fire causes heat and fever illness, so the soul causes the body to be alive, and this in every case. Death is the opposite of life, but the 'soul ... will never admit the opposite of that which it brings with it.'[33] That which does not admit death is immortal. So the soul is immortal.

The soul is here defined as the principle of life, as fire is the principle of heat, and hence is the opposite of cold. Plato's conclusion is that the soul as the principle of life does not admit of the idea of its opposite, namely death. But, as we have already seen, Plato speaks of the soul in two different ways. To prove the eternity of soul defined in one way does not entail the eternity of soul defined differently. Specifically, when (if he has done so) Plato proves that the soul as the principle of life is eternal, he has not shown that the soul as the individual human person is immortal.

Nevertheless, Plato did take 'soul' to mean the essential person, the real self, as for example in his report of the death of Socrates, the man. In answer to Crito's question, 'How shall we bury you?' which he asked Socrates on the day of his execution[34], Socrates replied: 'After I drink the poison, I shall no longer be with you.' His point was that when his body would be disposed of, he, Socrates, would not be there. For his soul, that is to say, his essential self, would escape. So, in answer to Crito's question, as to how he should bury him, Socrates replied, 'However you please, if you can

---

33 *Phaedo*, 115C-E.
34 The Greeks allowed the condemned prisoner to drink the poison at any time he chose during the day of execution, and permitted him to entertain his friends during that day.

catch me and I do not get away from you.'[35] His soul, which was his essential self, would escape from his body at death, and 'he,' the real Socrates, would no longer be there. They would bury the body, but would not catch *him*. He would have moved to his new and immortal existence.

We can summarise the arguments Plato employs in the *Phaedo*:

(1) The Cyclical Argument, or the *Argument from Reciprocal Processes*. Plato's method is (1) to establish a general principle of generation from opposites; (2) to apply the principle to the case under consideration, namely the living and the dead; (3) to derive the conclusion that there is a process of the living coming from the dead.

(2) The *Argument from Recollection*. The aim here is to show that the Forms are different things from the things which remind us of them. For example, the Forms are not variable. The things which remind us of them are. We are conscious of such lack of similarity.

(3) The *Argument from Affinity*. This is an argument by analogy. The soul is like the Forms in such and such respects. Therefore it is like the Forms in others. There are three lines of approach: (a) What is constant and invariable is likely to be *incomposite*. The absolutes, e.g. absolute equality and things of that sort, e.g. Forms, can hardly be supposed to vary. Particular instances, e.g. of equality, do vary. The variables are perceived by the senses. The invariables can be apprehended only by reason. The soul is more akin to the class of things that are invisible and so *invariable*. (b) When seeking truth all by itself the soul suffers no confusion. When the soul uses the senses in seeking knowledge it is confused, is presented with things that change. Therefore the soul is likely to be incomposite and therefore *immortal*.[36] (c) The soul's nature is to rule, the body's to serve. So the soul is more *akin to the divine*.

Plato then provided a final proof arguing that the Forms are 'causes.' The Forms are the only true causes. To give an account

---

35 *Phaedo*, 115C-E.
36 *Phaedo*, 69E-71E; 72E-78B; 78B-84B.

of the hypothesis one uses in explanation one needs to provide a further hypothesis, a 'higher' one, i.e. formulate a notion of a more comprehensive Form which explains the original hypothesis.[37]

Plato provided other arguments for the immortality of the soul, for example the argument from motion. He distinguished between those things which were moved from outside themselves and those things which had the principle of movement within themselves. The soul is self-moved, not requiring anything from without to move it. What moves because the principle of motion is within itself has a soul. So the soul is 'ungenerated and immortal.' Since the soul is not generated, its immortality stretches backward as well as forward. Hence the soul existed before this human existence. The previous existence of the soul was not one of inactivity. The soul's activity is one of contemplation, of learning. So in its pre-existent state, the soul contemplated the eternal ideas. It collected knowledge. Plato's teaching of the soul was very closely related to his theory of knowledge. So he believed that knowledge was 'wholly recollection.' One remembered, one recalled, what one had learned in a previous existence.

5 *MENO:* KNOWLEDGE IS REMEMBERING

He demonstrated (to his own satisfaction) in his dialogue *Meno* that knowledge was a remembering. The subject he interrogates is the servant of his friend, Meno. He elicited geometrical knowledge from the slave boy, who had never heard of Pythagoras' theorem. But when Socrates questioned him, he gave the correct answer. Plato concluded that the slave boy's knowledge was a remembering of what his soul had learned in a previous existence, since he had not learned it in this one. That being the case, the soul existed before we were born. Hence the soul is immortal. The doctrine of the immortality of the soul is confirmed for Plato by such considerations about the problem of knowledge. Knowledge is reminiscence.

---

37 *Phaedo,* 95E-102A.

At death the separation of the soul from the body takes place. The soul which began the pursuit of knowledge in this bodily existence can than pursue its quest without the drag of the body. Death then is the point of release of soul from body, for only after death can the soul 'be by itself apart from the body, but not before.' The true philosopher practices dying and death has no fears for him, since the moment of death is the moment of purification, the moment of release, The soul can now live 'alone by itself, freed from the body as from fetters.'[38]

---

[38] *Phaedo*, 65A-68A.

VI Aristotle's Functionalism

1 Aristotle's question.

Aristotle developed his own vocabulary for dealing with the soul. It looks somewhat forbidding, but his underlying explanation is relatively simple. Aristotle asks the question, 'What is the soul?' The answer he gives is in general terms. So he asks, 'How do persons differ from other material things in the world?' For human beings are material beings. They share with plants and animals features that mark off living things from non-living things. So plants, animals and human beings have life. As living things they reproduce and they nourish themselves by appropriate means.[39]

In answering the question he asked, 'What is it to be a person?' Aristotle took account of the many different things he observed that persons do, as well as the many different things which things other than persons do, and he made a contrast between the different kinds of thing. But he also noticed and noted the kinds of thing common to both, those things which persons and non-persons (such as plants and animals) do. The question can be put in another way, 'How shall we speak of body and soul in relation to the living body of persons?'

2 Different kinds of activity

He observed that there were different *kinds* of thing human beings did. They run and dig. But they also remember and make judgments. They eat, but they also solve mathematical problems. They get physical pleasure from eating. But they also get intellectual satisfaction from reasoning. They see impressive sights, and the senses are gratified. They work our intellectual problems and this provides a different, and for him, a higher kind of satisfac-

---

39 Sources from which this chapter draws are Aristotle, *De Anima*, I, II. 1-4

tion, what he calls *eudaimonia*, roughly translated 'happiness.' So persons are complicated beings. But how shall we consider the relation between body and soul, or mind (*psuche* in Greek)?

So we have two basic questions:

(1) What distinguishes persons from other material things?
(2) What is the relation between soul and body in human persons, in these beings which, like those with whom they contrast, are also material things?

3 Two Defining Statements

To answer these questions Aristotle defines what he understands by soul (*psuche*). In doing so he engages in criticising the teachings of his mentor, Plato. We shall start with two terse and apparently enigmatic statements he makes about the soul. The first is an analogy. The second is a definition.

'If the eye were an animal, sight would be its soul.'

'The soul is the first actuality of a natural body which potentially has life.'

Aristotle provides two sets of distinctions in expounding and explaining. The first is between the *stuff* out of which something is made, on the one hand, and the *shape* it is given so that it ends up by being the particular thing that it is. For example: Here is a piece of marble. The sculptor works with it, and provides a shape, so that the piece of marble now emerges as a statue, a work of art. What it was not (a work of art) it has now come to be, by virtue of the form the artist has given it. So there has been a passage from lump of stuff to work of art. What has made the difference is the form the artist gave to the material. This is a process.

So we can now introduce a second set of terms. The marble had the capacity to be transformed into a work of art. The sculptor has the capacity to transform the raw stuff into a piece of art. So what was potential becomes actual. Indeed, the idea of becoming involves the realizing of some potentiality the thing has. The po-

Death, Immortality, and Resurrection

tential becomes the actual. The matter is given a form. The marble which has the potential to become a work of art actually becomes one. The man who has the potentiality to become an artist actually becomes one. In both cases there is a movement from potentiality to actuality. So *potentiality* and *actuality* are key terms for Aristotle, not the least in his explanation of what soul, *psuche*, is.

But how do we know whether something has potential? We can know whether something has a potential by observing what it becomes. We can see the statue emerging from the marble. We can see the form taking shape. We observe form being imposed on the matter. We judge what was potential by observing what is actual. Aristotle used his own language for these phenomena. He speaks of *first actuality* and *second actuality*. By *first actuality* he means what we call potentiality, what something may become and by *second actuality* he means what we call actuality, what it has in fact become.

For the fact is that the potentiality may not be actualised. Something that has the capacity to cut, for example, may never cut. For Aristotle, a thing is defined in terms of its potentiality. An axe for example is defined in terms of its capacity to cut and chop. The thing I see may look no different from an axe that can chop and cut. But this thing I see can't do those things. It is rusty. Its blade is broken, ill fitting and its handle worn and worm-eaten. So since the thing can't cut and chop, it is not an axe. If we call it an axe that is only as it were by courtesy. It's a quite different thing from the thing that can demonstrate its potential by actually cutting. Or that could do so, even if it never does.

4 ANALOGY OF THE EYE

Now for a look at Aristotle's analogy of the eye. 'If the eye were an animal, sight would be its soul' (*De Anima*, 412b 18-19). He is saying that what sight is to the eye in an animal, so something is to the soul in a human person. So if we figure out the relation between the eye and sight, we have the key to the understanding of soul and person. Sight is a capacity which could not be without the eye. Sight is not a something that can exist without the eye. It is not a substance. That is to say it is not an independently existing thing, a 'this something.' Nor, on the other hand, is the thing an eye if it cannot see, any more than the thing is an axe if it cannot cut. So we shall not think of the member of the corpse as an eye, even if it is no different in appearance from the eye in a living animal. It does not function. So it is not an eye. It functions, and seeing is its function, sight the result, so it is an eye. Eye is defined by seeing. The eye's function is to see. Seeing is the function of the eye. If there is no such functioning, there is nothing worthy to be called 'eye.' If there is no potential for such functioning, there is no eye.

Just as the eye is a set of capacities summed up by the term 'sight', so soul is a set of capacities. We said earlier that human beings are material beings. What then is there about this matter that makes it unique? For Aristotle, this is the crucial question. What capacities, potentialities, does this 'parcel of matter' have which makes it distinctively human? What distinguishes the human soul from the souls of animals and plants? For Aristotle thinks of soul as 'principle of life.' The answer he gives is in terms of its potentialities. So he calls 'soul (*psuche*),' 'the first actuality (i.e. potentiality) of a natural body (i.e. a material thing) which potentially has life.'

5 Soul is not separable from body

That means that soul is not something separate from body. It is not another thing, another kind of thing, a non-material thing. This is in stark opposition to Plato's teaching of the separateness of the soul from the body, of soul as opposed to the material, and as the real essence of the human. For Plato the soul could escape the body when the body died and achieve its true end thereafter. There is nothing of the kind with Aristotle. Soul is bound up with body. There is no non-material essence to escape. For the soul is the body in its distinctive human functioning. *Psyche* is not a separately existing something in addition to the body. It is the set of capacities, potentialities, the body has, the *first actuality* of the body.

Death, Immortality, and Resurrection

Aristotle's question is 'What can a thing do?' Where the thing is the human person, the question is what are the things the *psuche* is capable of doing? We can give examples of what the mind does, as we observe it in exercise. It can think, e.g. remember, solve problems. It can feel, produce a feeling response to the things around it. Such capacities distinguish it from things on the lower orders of being like statues, knives etc. Aristotle had used analogies from inanimate things to illustrate the relation he wished to propose between body and soul. He rejected the view that body and soul were two things. He proposed that there were two sets of events, bodily and mental, physical on the one hand, what we might dub '*psuche*-ical' on the other. The problem now is to say in what way these are related. To what extent do the analogical instances help us in understanding the capacities of the living?

6 Aristotle's materialism

A kind of materialism marks Aristotle off from Plato (and from Descartes later. See below). Aristotle wrote: 'Since then the complex here is the living thing, the body cannot be the actuality of the soul. It is the soul which is the actuality of a certain kind of body .... the soul cannot be without the body, while it cannot *be* a body; it is not a body, but something relative to a body' (*De Anima*, 414 a 19-20).

As sight, i.e. the capacity to see, cannot exist without the eye, since a capacity requires something to have the capacity (this is the general principle), so (1) the soul, *psuche*, cannot exist without the body. But Aristotle hastens to add (2) the soul is not the body. The body is not the set of capacities, of potentialities. There is a difference between the knife and the capacity to cut. We do not call the knife 'the capacity to cut.' So there is a difference between the body and the capacity the body has to reproduce and to think. This capacity, or set of capacities, is the soul. So we cannot call the body the capacity to reproduce and to think. We cannot identify the soul with the body. Using the other terminology, we can say that the soul is the form of the body. This enables us to recognise that just as the statue is a combination of matter and form, and that here the form is not separable from the matter, so in the case of the human person, the non-material capacities define the human. Those non-material capacities are being the *form* of the human and so are not separable from it. Just as you can't talk about the statue without talking about the matter, (but the statue is not the form separated from the matter,) so you cannot talk about the human person without talking about the material, the body. But the soul is not separable from the matter. It not the form separated from the matter.

7 FUNCTIONS COMMON AND UNIQUE.

We should now make explicit what has been implied in our earlier exposition. The body is matter and therefore potentiality. The form, or first actuality, first *entelechy* of the person, is the *psuche*. Here Aristotle is speaking of the *several* capacities the body has, its dispositions, tendencies. What is to be noted here is that by *psuche* Aristotle speaks not only of the intellectual capacities but also of natural capacities, such as generation, perception, appetite. The human person shares these with animals, and in the case of generation with plants. The second actuality is the actual exercise of the capacities and dispositions, as seen in the events and processes which the person exercises and manifests. Thus Aristotle, in his comprehensive theory of the soul, can recognise both those capacities human beings have uniquely, and those which they share with the lower things that have life.

VII Cartesian Dualism

1 Man more than body

Descartes (AD 1596 - 1650), sometimes called the father of modern philosophy, was a dualist. He taught that soul and body are quite distinct realities. When we examine his arguments, we find ourselves in a quite different world from that of Plato, with whom he has kinship and who (as we have seen) was also a dualist. Descartes was a brilliant mathematician and a competent scientist. He was a mechanist. That means that he thought of bodies as machines. He was also a convinced Christian believer. So he affirmed that God had created the souls of men and this made them different from the animals. For animals are merely machines. They have no soul. Human beings have souls in the bodily machine.

So while he was excited about the discovery and researches of William Harvey, who had discovered the circulation of the blood, and whose work on the heart had been published in AD 1628, Descartes did not consider that all of human behaviour was simply physical and mechanical. There was in human behaviour what could not be accounted for in bodily language. Man was more than body. To account for this more than bodily activity he spoke of mind, soul or understanding. His great problem, once he had separated and radically distinguished body from soul, was to explain how they operated.[40]

Of the body he writes: 'the body is ... a machine ... made by the hands of God' (127). But man is distinguished from the animals in possessing reason, which disposes his actions in ways different from that of the animals. The 'rational soul' of which man is possessed is not derived from matter but is 'expressly created' by God. No matter can account for mind. That is Descartes' principle. So

---

[40] References are again, for convenience, to Flew, *op. cit.*

what 'we cannot ... conceive as possibly pertaining to a body, must be attributed to our soul' (22). 'The rational soul ... could not be in any way derived from the power of matter ... but ... it must be expressly created' (129). He takes this principle for granted and it serves as the basis for several arguments.

2 THE METHOD OF DOUBT

A well-known argument of Descartes is called his method of doubt. He decided that he would doubt all that he could possibly doubt. He asked what would happen if an evil demon would set out to deceive him. Was there anything that the demon could not convince Descartes that he could doubt? When the demon had done his work, was there anything indubitable left? Descartes' answer was that the evil genius might convince him that the external world was a dream. But there were some things Descartes could not doubt. So Descartes' method of doubt led him to something certain beyond doubt. There remained something that he could not doubt. When he tried to doubt his previous certainties, he came to the conclusion that while he could indeed doubt most of them, there was one thing which was indubitable. That was that he was doubting. Descartes doubted first one original certainty and then another original certainty. In the process of doubting Descartes realised that *he*, Descartes, was doubting. Of that he was certain. He was doubting. Since he was doubting, Descartes was thinking. For doubting is a form of thinking. He had now come to rock bottom certainty, the certainty that he was thinking. He could now draw a further conclusion. Since he was certain that he was thinking, he was certain that he existed. So he believed that he now had a foundation upon which he could build a system of thought. At the basis of this system was an indubitable certainty.

That is not the end of his argument. He now asks about the 'I' that thinks. What is this self? The answer he gives to that question leads him to the question of immortality.

Death, Immortality, and Resurrection   109

When he has established that he exists, for to doubt means to think and to think means to exist, he can then ask *what* he is. In giving his answer he takes a big step. His answer is that he is 'a thing which thinks,' 'a mind or a soul, or an understanding, or a reason' (132). The self is a thinking thing. The essential self, the real self, is the mind or the soul.

3 Soul — the thinking thing

Now he moves to another stage in the argument. Since Descartes has a clear idea that he is a thinking and unextended thing, and since he has a clear idea that his body, in contrast, is 'only an extended and unthinking thing,' what follows for him is that since (to use his words) 'I am a thinking thing ... this I (that is to say Descartes' soul, by which he is the "I" he is), is entirely and absolutely distinct from my body, and can exist without it' (132: parentheses supplied).

The real self, the real person, is the soul, which is housed within the body. The body is a mechanical system of interrelated parts. The soul or mind is, in this life, joined to the body only for as long as the body lives. It is when bodily functions cease that death comes and never 'by reason of the soul' (138). The distinction between body and soul is pressed further. The body ceases to function at death. So since the soul is the antithesis of the body, that antithesis can be extended to take us beyond the death of the body.

The body dies. The soul does not. It lives on. It can do so because it is different from the body and so 'it is not liable to die with it' (129). This leads Descartes to the conclusion that the soul is immortal. 'And then, inasmuch as we observe no other causes capable of destroying it, we are naturally inclined to judge that it is immortal' (129).

Descartes began with the assumption that the body, a material machine, cannot be responsible for thought. Since the bodily machine cannot think, which for Descartes means to display the characteristics of consciousness, and since human beings do display the characteristics of consciousness, there must be an essential self, a real self, that is responsible for this consciousness.

But then a serious problem arises. To separate soul (mind) from body means that it is difficult to show that there is some relation between them, and the more radical the separation or distinction the greater the difficulty, But thinking goes on within the body. So there must be some connection between the soul and the body, if the soul expresses itself through the body. How does it do this unless there is at some point a contact between the immaterial soul (mind) and the material body? If the soul is quite other than the body, it would seem we face an impossibility. How is it possible that two such opposites could be in relation to one another?

4 Mind separate from body?

Descartes tries to meet this difficulty. The soul is one and since it is indivisible it does not exist in any part of the body. By saying this he preserves the separateness of the mind from the body. But soul (mind) exercises its functions more particularly in an inward part of the brain, in 'the small gland which is the main seat of the soul' (142). But how does it do this? That is an empirical question. By making this adventurous additional assertion, Descartes was attempting to give a good account of his original assumption that the non-bodily activities have to be accounted for in other than bodily terms. The non-bodily activities in question are mental activities, thinking in its many forms, e.g. remembering, calculating, reasoning. He was offering a testable hypothesis when he pointed to the pineal gland as the physical point at which soul influences body.

What Descartes' assumption means (24) is that the words we use of mental activity, mental terms, have no connection with the words we use of bodily activity. This assumption is false. That being so, we cannot accept the dualism Descartes sets up between body and soul (mind). Since his doctrine of the immortality of the soul is based on that foundation, it is shown to be untenable.

The psycho-physical unity of the person is an empirical fact.

Death, Immortality, and Resurrection

Descartes has a pair of difficulties at this point. The two questions we can ask are complementary. First, How does a particular immaterial event produce a physical result? For example, How does something in the mind (conceived on Cartesian lines) cause the physical event of my turning my head, or my lifting my arm? Second, How does a physical event cause mental, i.e. immaterial events? How does something that takes place in the body produce something in the mind? For example: How does a blow on the head produce pain? The blow is a physical event. The pain is a mental event. Can we even conceive a notion of cause between such radical opposites as on a Cartesian view?[41]

Gilbert Ryle in his book, *The Concept of Mind*, argued against Descartes' view that body and mind are two quite different sorts of reality, that there is a realm of physical things and a realm of mental things, quite separate from one another. Descartes had taught that there was a whole separate world of non-physical activities, what he called 'thought.' He meant the term 'thought' to be taken in a broad sense. For him it means 'consciousness'.[42]

5 CATEGORY MISTAKE

A special language grew up to refer to this private world of thought, and to the varied activities which went on in it. 'Mind' and 'soul' were key words in this vocabulary. Ryle attacked the whole idea of a private mental world and its accompanying concepts. He held that such words do not refer to some 'thing,' some entity alongside of or in addition to the agent's behaviour. There are no inner, private, mental worlds in addition to the common world of physical things. To talk as if there were is to make a fundamental mistake. Ryle calls it a *category mistake*, a mistake of language. One may not speak of 'mind' as something within, something which is

---

41 For more detailed criticism, see Peter Smith and O.R. Jones, *The Philosophy of Mind*. Cambridge: Cambridge University Press, 1988. pp. 31-69.
42 Gilbert Ryle, *The Concept of Mind*. London: Hutchinson, 1949. References in the text are to this work.

the source of the events internal to the private individual. To do so is to think of it as a kind of ghostly activity within the life of the body. Such 'mental-conduct concepts' are quite mistaken.

To hold such a view of mind leads to what Ryle has called pejoratively 'the dogma of the ghost in the machine' (15-16). Such dualism of body and soul (mind) is a category mistake, a philosopher's myth. One uses, or rather misuses, ideas suited to one context by placing them in another context for which they are not at all suited. One takes them as having the same meaning in the unsuitable context as they had in their original and appropriate context. So he defines 'myth' as 'the presentation of facts belonging to one category in the idioms appropriate to another'(8). That might be all right provided you recognise that you are using language figuratively and suggestively in the new context. It is a serious mistake if you think the language has the same meaning in its new context as it had in the old. The misuse of words then has betrayed you into thinking that there are actual entities which correspond to the words which you use.

That was Descartes' mistake. He said rightly that the body is a material thing. Bodily movements are causes and effects. The body is (according to Descartes) a machine. The body is a 'complex organised unit' (18). The mistake Descartes made was to use the same idiom of the mind. It is an error to hold, 'Minds are things, but different sorts of things from bodies. Mental processes are causes and effects, but different sorts of causes and effects from bodily movements .... As the human body is a complex organised unit, so the human mind must be a complex organised unity though one made of a different sort of stuff and with a different sort of structure' (18).

Put in a word, what Ryle says against Descartes is that you cannot talk of mind as if it were a thing, a different sort of thing from a material thing, but a thing nevertheless. It is unintelligible to speak as if, in addition to the body which is a thing, there is another thing, but of a different sort. We do not need to do that

Death, Immortality, and Resurrection

to account for human activity. 'Mind' is not a word for a thing. So it is not a name for a thing of a different sort than body.

So Ryle denies that 'There occur mental processes' means the same thing as 'There occur physical processes.' While the form of the sentence is the same in each case, the two sentences mean different things. They are just not saying similar things. If we think that they are we have been deceived by the use of the language.

What then does it mean to talk of a person's mind? Ryle answers, 'It is to talk of the person's abilities, liabilities and inclinations to do and undergo certain sorts of things, and of the doing and undergoing of these things in the ordinary world' (199). There is no shadowy entity within the physical organism. Mind language refers to human behaviour. But Ryle is quick to point out that to say this does not mean that man is a machine. 'Man need not be degraded to a machine by being denied to be a ghost in a machine' (328).

Nor does the rejection of the dualist view of the soul as a kind of thing mean that you may not talk of the soul at all. You can do it in a different way from the dualists. The soul is not a *part* of the person, and the term cannot be used in that way after Ryle's criticism. But that does not mean that you cannot use the term 'soul.' We do use it. We call people 'souls.' We call a person a 'soul,' 'a good soul,' 'a worthy soul,' 'a poor soul.' What we mean then is that that person has certain capacities.

Behaviourism is the view that what is called 'mind' is explicable in terms of the capacities which the human person has and exercises. We may use the terms 'soul' and 'mind,' but doing so does not commit us to a belief in a thing that exists separate from the physical processes. We exhaust mental talk by speaking of capacities. The question then is whether the behaviourist speaks adequately enough in such terms. He may not be doing so.

The reader will note a similarity between the Aristotelian criticisms of Plato's idealistic dualism and these which Ryle (and others) have been asking of Descartes' dualism.

VIII Replicas and Resurrection

1 Imagining, reflecting, understanding

We sometimes imagine situations that do not at present exist to find out what we think what we might do, how we might react. We consider alternative possibilities, for example, for the future, so as to help us in making decisions in the present. We also consider fictional situations to help us in making judgments. If I were placed in situation x ... what would I do? If such-and such were the case what would be the outcome? Then as we reflect on the decisions we might make, think how we might choose to act, we may come to understand better the kind of person we are.

We often do this profitably when considering a problem. We ask, If such-and-such were to be the case what would we think about it? How would we react to it? What judgments would we make about it?

Philosophers do this too. They create imagined situations and ask, 'What would we make of them?' They ask the question we have raised: 'What does the continued existence of a person consist in?' Put concretely, for example: 'What is it necessary for us to say that Mary is the same self or person now that she was twenty years ago?' We can then, quite profitably, imagine situations or possibilities which lead us to give different answers to the question. We can then evaluate the answers available to us. So let us ask, 'What makes a person at two different times one and the same person?' The two different times may be within our present existence, or it may be that the one time is now, in the present life, the other time after death. For the answer we give will apply equally to both. So imagine the following:

Mary has no memory of her former life.

Mary the princess remembers only the events of Jean the pauper's life.

A person with a body exactly resembling Jean's has only memories of Mary's life.

Mary disappears from New York and a body in all respects resembling hers appears in London.

Mary dies in New York and a body exactly resembling hers appears in London.

Mary dies in New York. Her body disappears, and a body exactly resembling hers and having the same memories as hers appears in London.

Mary enters a teletransportation machine which encodes her here and sends the message to a machine on another planet which decodes her there, producing a replica of Mary on another planet. She has the choice either to continue to exist here as well as being replicated, or, having been replicated, not to exist here.

Mary dies here and a body exactly resembling hers and having her memories appears on another planet.

So much for imagined situations. How do they help us with our problems about personal identity and resurrection?

2 IDENTITY: TWO MEANINGS

We must first make an important distinction. It concerns the meaning of 'same.' This is the distinction between *numerical identity* and *qualitative identity*. If I say to my students, 'Bring along the same book that I am using,' what I mean is that twenty students will each bring along one book each. Each of these books will have the same features as mine. They will have the same number of pages, same words on page one, two, three etc. They will be *qualitatively* identical. But if I say, holding up a particular book, 'This is the same book as the one I brought along last week,' I may mean something different by 'same.' I mean that it is the very one and no other. It is numerically the same book. It is numerically identical with the one I brought last week. I am referring to only one object. This is *numerical* identity. There is only one object in view here. The object is the same with itself over time.

So what is the question we are asking when we talk about personal sameness, or identity? Is it numerical or is it qualitative identity? Which one, if we must choose, or if we feel we must choose, is the appropriate idea when we are speaking of survival of death? Does it matter which? If we insist that we be the same persons after death as we were before, do we mean that we must be numerically identical, or are we satisfied with being qualitatively identical? But since we are bodily creatures what would it mean to be numerically identical after death with the same person as we were before death? Perhaps we should then speak not so much of identity but of continuity, physical and psychological.

3 REPLICATION

An interesting proposal for interpreting resurrection as replication has been made by John Hick. Does such an interpretation satisfy the religious hope for a future life?

Hick presents his 'replica' theory in his book *Death and Eternal Life*,[43] in the chapter on the Resurrection. If we reject a dualistic understanding of the soul, and hence the existence of the soul as an incorporeal thing, we will raise the question of life after death in a new way. Is it *possible* to conceive of continuity between the present person and the future person after death? Can we think it? Is it logically possible to think of identity between person one before death and person two after death? Are they in some sense 'one'? If we can conceive the possibility, we can go on thinking about it. Otherwise it is inconceivable and so we must stop thinking about it. If the identity of a resurrected person with a person who has lived in this life is conceivable, that is to say if it is logically possible, it will then be profitable to consider its real possibility, to ask whether it could actually be.

---

43 References in the text are to John Hick, *Death and Eternal Life*. London: Collins, 1976.

What makes the resurrection life of interest to the believer is that it is possible that it will be the same person's life that ended here on earth. But how can this be understood? Resurrection is not resuscitation, that is to say, the revival of the same body which died. Survival of the same body would not ensure immortality of the same person. Since resurrection does not mean the physical continuity of the same body which died, what other kind of continuity between this life and the resurrection life is it possible to conceive? Is it possible to conceive any? Is it possible to speak of identity without speaking of physical continuity?

As we have seen the term 'same' is used in two ways. I speak of reading the same book as you, when there are two books, in fact thousands of the same book. I do not mean when I say 'the same book' that there is only one. What I mean is that the book you are reading and the book I am reading are *qualitatively* identical, i.e. alike in all respects. The term 'same' is also used in the sense of *numerical* identity. In a police investigation, for instance, it may be a question of establishing whether this book is the same book as the one that was in a particular room at a particular time. 'Same' here means 'numerically identical' or 'one and the same.' To be 'one and the same,' 'numerically identical,' means to be in no respect different. So you can connote that and no other book: torn on page sixty-two, ink stain on the back cover, a signature in identifiable handwriting on the title page. There can be only one. The question of identity arises when this 'same' thing is perceived on different occasions.

Qualitative identity in contrast is of more than one thing. (Of course a numerically identical thing is qualitatively identical with itself, at least in some respect(s).) Two things (or more) are one in this sense. But two things that are one, 'the same' in this sense, are more than one in being two. So they are different in that they are plural.

If the resurrection life is not numerically or physically identical with this one, what other alternative is there? Can we speak of identity in a different and at the same time satisfactory way? Can we

Death, Immortality, and Resurrection

conceive of personal identity without requiring material continuity between the person who died and the person who lives immortally?

If we reject the dualistic understanding of soul and body, and accept the fact that the human person is a psycho-physical unity, and the fact that at death such unity ceases, what shall we say of the possibility of life after death? The alternatives are two. Either death is the end, or it is not. If God should perform a creative act then it is possible to hope for resurrection. If we believe God will perform such an act the problem is to see if and how we can intelligently think today of the resurrection body and of the process by which it comes into being.

John Hick proposes that we think of it 'as the divine creation in another space of an exact psycho-physical replica' of the deceased person' (279). A 'replica' (note the inverted commas) is not a replica. By 'replica,' Hick means that there is only one specimen. He assumes a non-numerical identity. 'Replica' means 'same' in the sense of qualitative identity, but with a qualification. How many identical things can there be? If 'same' means 'numerically identical,' there can be, by definition, only one. If 'same' means 'in all respects exactly similar' there still may be only one. For Hick, 'replica' means something in all respects exactly similar to something else, there being only one. The resurrected person is identical, in a non-numerical sense, with the person who lived. There is only one recreated self. Thus Hick refuses the possibility that God might simultaneously replicate the same person more than once. The idea that there might be several simultaneously existing same persons leads to quite interesting problems!

The addition of inverted commas suggests that the term is being used in a special sense. The one 'replica' is so 'exactly similar to him (the person who died), in all respects' (283), that we can regard the 'replica' as the same person as the original person. In this way, Hick feels that he can allow for the Christian teaching of resurrection and make intelligible the notion of identity, without relying upon dualistic assumptions.

4 Three pictures

So, we must establish minimum criteria for saying that Y is the same person as X. Hick invites us to consider three 'pictures.' Person Y disappears in London and an exact 'replica' of Y appears in New York. If this happened we would, after due consideration, say that the 'replica' in New York was the 'same' person as the one who disappeared in London.

A second case is that of Y dying suddenly in London and with his dead body in London, an exact 'replica' of him appears in New York. The 'replica' is of the man he was before his death, physically and psychologically, specifically with respect to his memories. We would in these unusual circumstances use the term 'same person' of the 'replica' in New York. We would, of course, make sure that he was conscious of being the same person who had previously lived and died in London. What we would then be doing would be to give the term 'same' or 'identical' as now used of the person a new meaning that it did not have before, because the circumstances which occasion the new use had not arisen before. That would by no means be an unusual linguistic phenomenon.

The third picture is of Y dying and his 'replica' appearing in a resurrected world inhabited by resurrected 'replicas.' This 'replica' is a psycho-physical reality, not a disembodied soul (285). There would be sufficient evidence in such a situation, the situation of existing in another world (in another space, says Hick) for Y to identify himself as the same person he had been before his death. The evidence for such identity would be of the same sort which enables one to identify oneself and other people in the present existence, and in the other unusual cases considered.

He would have the same memory in the resurrection world as in this one and also a similar psycho-physical unity. In some sense he has the same body then as now. He has, moreover, the consciousness of being the same person, 'same' in that he has been created a 'replica,' 'same' in the sense of qualitative not numerical identity.

Death, Immortality, and Resurrection

The purpose for which Hick has presented these three 'pictures' is to suggest how we might intelligently think of the resurrection body today (279). Such a philosophical exercise is demanded if our modern understanding of man as 'an indissoluble psycho-physical unity,' as an 'empirical self,' is to be taken as the basis for consideration of the possibility of life after death. Such a suggestion, assuming the psycho-physical unity of man, means that there is no room for the notion of soul as an entity in distinction from body. If there is no soul in distinction from body, there can be no question of the soul surviving the death of the body. Hence the need to present an intelligible conception of what life after death might be, while denying the traditional dualism.

5 Qualitative identity

Hick wishes to establish the logical possibility of life after death, while at the same time rejecting the existence of the soul as a separate entity. To establish that logical possibility is to show that the conception is intelligible. Hick has done this, whatever the difficulties of his position. That being the case, we may feel free to proceed and explore the possibilities which 'resurrection of the person' opens up for theological construction.

If we have established the *logical* possibility of speaking of the person resurrected in a different world as the same person as the one who lived on this earth, we can then go on and ask about the *real* possibility. Not everything that is logically possible happens. If there is to be a resurrection it will be, according to Christian belief, because God raises the dead. The *real* possibility depends upon God. The belief that there will be a resurrection of the dead involves belief in a certain kind of God. Grounds for belief in such a God can then be considered as grounds for the resurrection of the dead at the last day.

Our question must now be whether such an interpretation of resurrection and survival in terms of qualitative identity satisfies the religious hope. We have seen that it presents us with an alternative to two other interpretations, namely that of cessation of all life at death, and the dualistic proposal of disembodied soul.

If this is the one logical possibility which is compatible with the Christian belief that God graciously gives life after death, and enables us to understand how this might be so, when other alternatives are not satisfactory, then it would seem that it is rational to accept the suggestion. Derek Parfit, from whom the discussion has taken its cue, has an interesting analogy.[44] Numerical identity is not possible, he says, after discussing the imagined teletransportation cases, in one of which the replicated person exists simultaneously with the original person. It is not possible that two things are numerically identical. Numerical identity means that a thing at time^{two} is in no way different from the thing at time^{one}. There is only *one* thing. Qualitative identity means that *two* things at the same or at different times are identical. The resurrected person is qualitatively identical with the person that lived pre-mortem.

Suppose that you lost your sight and that scientists developed an artificial, electronic, eye that functioned in all respects like your original eyes. You now have two implanted eyes and they function to give you all the capacities your old eyes ever had. Moreover suppose they look the same as your old eyes. (Here we depart from Parfit's example). It is in fact a case of replication. Would there be any reason why you should not be content? Why should you wish for more? Even if, as in Parfit's example, the artificial eyes did not have the appearance of normal eyes, they would be as good as normal sight. It would not be plausible to reject these eyes because they were not the normal cause of human sight. Nor, argues Parfit, in the case of the teletransported construction of the replica, would it be plausible to reject him. He is like me in every way, with a normal brain and body. So of the recreated person whom God creates as replica of the person who lived. Reconstruction provides for the same person to exist.

---

44 Derek Parfit, *Reasons and Persons*, Oxford: The Clarendon Press, 1987. p. 285.

Additional Note

Life after Life. A Review of Raymond A Moody's Book.

While the statement on the cover claims that there are 'actual case histories that reveal there is life after death,' the author who undoubtedly chose the title of the book *Life after Life* deliberately, carefully avoids making such a claim, and in his closing pages specifically repudiates it.' I would insist,' he writes 'that I am not under the delusion that I have 'proven' there is life after death' (p. 181). For him, as a philosopher, 'prove' is being used in the strong sense, as of a logical demonstration. He also makes clear that he does not wish to draw 'conclusions' nor to use his material as 'evidence' (pp. 182-183).

However, two pertinent observations conclude the writing. The first is that the data are such that only with a seriously revised understanding, logical and scientific, may we be able to do justice to them. The second is that his own psychological response, an affirmative one, leads him to hope that once the data are presented and considered the hypothesis that mind can exist apart from the body may make a difference to those who have dealings with the ones who face death. Thus the book has an interesting practical bearing.

The question is, 'What are we to make of the data the book presents?' These data point to the fact that a form of consciousness is possible in which the mind, while not entirely dissociated from the body — the presence of the body is obvious in the examples — nevertheless sustains a relationship to it which is quite different from that of normal experience. The 'subject' sees his body, and recognises that it is his body, at least at the outset of the experience.

The question must be raised as to the relevance of such experiences to the question about the state after death, *post mortem*. One might compare these experiences with those documented by Celia Green in her interesting book, *Out of the Body Experiences*. She here instances the fascination which the subject experiences at 'seeing' the 'physical body' still functioning as conditions permitted, as sleeping, or in a trance-like state, sick or injured. Here there is no question as to whether the body is 'dead' or 'dying.' It is not. What then is the relevance of either set of experiences to the problem of death and of life after death, when only in some instances is there a close brush with death? If in the one case there is no connection, why should there be in the other, except for the incident of the fact that the subject did in fact nearly die? There is an interesting overlap in the two sets of experience. The point is that out-of-the-body experiences are not confined to the dying. In some cases the near death experience is more complex, but not in all.

The fact is that one cannot interview the dead. All of Moody's cases are of people who had a critical circumstance that brought them to the point of death, or circumstances which might have ended in death. He says that in earlier periods they would have died (145), that they were closer to death than anyone else (152), both of which mean that they did not die. He recognises that none of his subjects were dead, if death is defined as a condition from which there is no return. To die and to be resuscitated is, on this definition, a contradiction of terms. We endorse this definition. So the position can be put in the form of an argument.

If we take the conditions for a near death experience as *analogous* to post mortem 'experience' (assuming the possibility of such experience for the sake of argument), we might then interpret the evidence as indicating that post mortem survival is probable. But there is no way of making the analogy good in the first instance. We cannot argue from state of non-death, i.e. a state from which there is a 'return,' to a state of death from which there is no return. If we start with a questionable premise (i.e. the cases are analogous), we shall end with a dubious conclusion (i.e. there is post mortem survival, out of the body). The argument that the near death state is analogous to the after death state and the near death state is one in which consciousness on a different level than normal takes place, therefore the post mortem state is a state of consciousness, is dubious because its premise is questionable.

But even if we start with the stronger assertion as premise, the desired conclusion does not follow.

These experiences are post mortem experiences,

Therefore, there is consciousness post-mortem,

The argument, if it does not express a tautology, is not valid. For these post-mortem experiences may be transitional. It still would have to be established that they were registers of the *total* post mortem state. This it is quite obviously not possible to demonstrate. No conclusions could be drawn from such transitional post mortem states to the total post mortem state. At the end of the transitional state, there may be non-consciousness.

Since this is the case with regard to such an argument for conscious survival, it is the case, *a fortiori*, if the argument is used for immortality.

But in fact the premise is false. These are not post-mortem experiences. They are pre-mortem experiences. Indeed since the subjects did not die, it is misleading to speak of 'life after life.' The expression is at best ambiguous, at worse misleading. For it gives the impression that life had ended. But this is not so. The experiences are pre-death experiences in unusual circumstances, since the subjects survived with death quite a way off.

Such considerations lead to the interesting question, 'What would constitute proof of life after death?' We cannot at any length here discuss the meaning of proof. Suffice it to say that the strong sense of proof is of logical demonstration. If one starts with a true premise, or true premises and argues logically, the conclusion follows i.e. is true, and is proved. So, in the Platonic tradition, it appears that immortality was proved since one started with the indubitable certainty that mind (soul) was other than body. But an indubitable certainty need not be true.

What was possible for Plato is no longer possible for us, namely to assert confidently that the soul is a substance, that is that soul is a separate and continuing reality. What has made the difference is evidence concerning the relationships between psychological and physical entities.

Another sense of 'prove' is that of appealing effectively to experience or to evidence, so that a high degree of probability is established which is taken, for all intents and purposes, as establishing the proposition in view. In this case it becomes a question of showing that a position is reasonable, in view of the fact that the same may be the case with alternative positions. F. H. Bradley commented with reference to the problem of survival, 'strictly to prove continuity is impossible and we must content ourselves with a certain probability' (in Antony Flew (editor), *Body, Mind and Death*. New York, 1973. p. 216). That, we would say, is the very most that one might expect from Moody's evidence. But, as we have seen, the evidence is questionable. It is, that is to say, open to alternative explanations, which *may* not all be exclusive.

We turn now to characteristics of the experience and end with observations on arguments from 'experience.'

First, the experiences are almost totally egocentric. When, for example, the subjects experienced the being of light, they focused their attention upon themselves. Their past life came under review. They felt happy and comfortable.

Second, a clear ethical dimension was lacking. There was nothing at all here like the Judgment of apocalyptic imagery. Everyone was accepted after 'death.' Even past misdeeds were received by the bright being of light with tolerance, even with humour. There is casualness in some of the descriptions of this encounter. It was fun going back on one's life in the experience of flashback.

Third, the experience was not beyond recall. While many of the subjects noted that they could not adequately describe what they had experienced, they nevertheless insisted that they could say quite a considerable number of reasonable things about the experience. It was not totally ineffable and the language of ordinary experience did not distort it. It was simply inadequate.

But what is the status of *any* appeal to experience? Can one argue from experience to what is beyond experience, in this case from experiences to conscious survival post mortem or to immortality? Note that we have not talked of arguing to God as the Guarantor of such survival.

Let us take the minimal claim, namely that people have had such experiences is evidence that such experiences are possible. We shall have quite enough to go on for the moment, the empirical moment, if we take account of this fact as seriously as we might. Moody himself observed that his line of approach was not the right one for the study of re-incarnation (142). But he did not affirm that it was the right mode for studying the problem of survival and immortality. Is it?

If we take the reports as true, i.e. if we take the experiences as veridical and as adequately reported, shall we conclude that we have interesting phenomena which bear on the mind-body problem (for example many of the experiences occurred to women in pregnancy) and which must be taken into account by any philosopher or doctor in assessing human capacities? Perhaps we do not know what before we thought we did and that old questions must be re-opened and new methods found for answering them. Moody suggests that we have here 'a novel phenomenon for which we may have to devise new modes of explanation and interpretation' (177). We may, in C. J. Ducasse's words, 'need to revise rather radically in some respects our ordinary ideas of what is and what is not possible in nature' (Flew, *op. cit.*, 228). The alternative is to dismiss the experiences as not significant. That it seems hard to do.

INDEX

A

Aristotle 90, 101, 102, 103, 104, 105, 106
Athanasius 31
Augustine 26, 73

B

Barrett, C.K. 85
Bradley, F.H. 126
Buber 46
Bultmann, Rudolph 49

C

Calvin 39, 64, 65, 69
Cullmann 41, 42, 43, 44

D

De Anima 101, 103, 105
Descartes 65, 90, 105, 107, 108, 109, 110, 111, 112, 113
Donne, John iii

F

Flew, Antony 93, 96, 107, 126, 127

G

Green, Celia 123

H

Hamlet 40
Hick, John 28, 62, 63, 68, 91, 117, 119, 120, 121

I

Irenaeus 35

J

Job 7

K

Kaufman, Gordon 18, 64, 69
Kohler, Ludwig 75

M

Meno 94, 99
Moody, Raymond A. 9, 123, 124, 126, 127

P

Parfit, Derek 122
Parmenides 94, 95
Paul 24, 25, 29, 30, 31, 33, 34, 35, 37, 42, 48, 82, 89
Penelhum, Terence 41, 76
Phaedo 96, 98
Pharisees 23, 24
Plato 17, 35, 61, 90, 93, 94, 95, 96, 97, 98, 99, 102, 105, 107, 125

R

Richardson, Alan 35, 36
Robinson, H. Wheeler 35, 45, 48, 85

S

Sadducees 23, 24
Scott, R.B.Y. 85
Socrates 57, 94, 99

T

Tolstoy 5

W

Watts, Isaac 56
Wiles, Maurice 76, 79

Y

Yahweh 37, 45, 85

ALSO FROM ENERGION PUBLICATIONS

Herold Weiss's meditations ... tease out Paul's theology buried in his authentic letters. And as a bonus, the book is a pleasure to read.

– **Rubén Dupertuis, Ph.D.**
Truinity University

ALSO BY DR. EDWARD W. H. VICK

As a tutor for believers who wish to enhance their understanding of how their faith stands under scrutiny, Philosophy for Believers is a unique resource. It is a serious bookfor serious readers.

Herold Weiss, Ph.D.
Professor Emeritus of New Testament, St. Mary's College, Notre Dame

MORE FROM ENERGION PUBLICATIONS

Personal Study

Finding My Way in Christianity	Herold Weiss	$16.99
Holy Smoke! Unholy Fire	Bob McKibben	$14.99
The Jesus Paradigm	David Alan Black	$17.99
When People Speak for God	Henry Neufeld	$17.99

Christian Living

Faith in the Public Square	Robert D. Cornwall	$16.99
Grief: Finding the Candle of Light	Jody Neufeld	$8.99
Crossing the Street	Robert LaRochelle	$16.99

Bible Study

Learning and Living Scripture	Lentz/Neufeld	$12.99
From Inspiration to Understanding	Edward W. H. Vick	$24.99
Philippians: A Participatory Study Guide	Bruce Epperly	$9.99
Ephesians: A Participatory Study Guide	Robert D. Cornwall	$9.99
Meditations on the Letters of Paul	Herold Weiss	$14.99

Theology

Creation in Scripture	Herold Weiss	$12.99
Creation: the Christian Doctrine	Edward W. H. Vick	$12.99
The Politics of Witness	Allan R. Bevere	$9.99
Ultimate Allegiance	Robert D. Cornwall	$9.99
History and Christian Faith	Edward W. H. Vick	$9.99
The Adventists' Dilemma	Edward W. H. Vick	$14.99
The Church Under the Cross	William Powell Tuck	$11.99
The Journey to the Undiscovered Country	William Powell Tuck	$9.99
Eschatology: A Participatory Study Guide	Edward W. H. Vick	$9.99

Ministry

Clergy Table Talk	Kent Ira Groff	$9.99
Thrive	Ruth Fletcher	$14.99

Generous Quantity Discounts Available
Dealer Inquiries Welcome
Energion Publications — P.O. Box 841
Gonzalez, FL_ 32560
Website: http://energionpubs.com
Phone: (850) 525-3916

www.ingramcontent.com/pod-product-compliance
Lightning Source LLC
LaVergne TN
LVHW041544070426
835507LV00011B/922